The Poet's Guide to Publish

The Poet's Guide to Publishing

*How to Conceive, Arrange,
Edit, Publish and Market
a Book of Poetry*

KATERINA STOYKOVA

McFarland & Company, Inc., Publishers
Jefferson, North Carolina

Library of Congress Cataloguing-in-Publication Data

Names: Stoykova, Katerina, author.
Title: The poet's guide to publishing : how to conceive, arrange, edit, publish
    and market a book of poetry / Katerina Stoykova.
Description: Jefferson, North Carolina : McFarland & Company, Inc., Publishers,
    2024. | Includes bibliographical references and index.
Identifiers: LCCN 2024024731 | ISBN 9781476694153
    (paperback : acid free paper) ∞
    ISBN 9781476652436 (ebook)
Subjects: LCSH: Poetry—Marketing—Handbooks, manuals, etc. | Poetry—
    Publishing—Handbooks, manuals, etc.
Classification: LCC PN1059.M3 S76 2024 | DDC 808.1—dc23/eng/20240627
LC record available at https://lccn.loc.gov/2024024731

British Library cataloguing data are available

ISBN (print) 978-1-4766-9415-3
ISBN (ebook) 978-1-4766-5243-6

Front cover image: © sunwart/Shutterstock

Printed in the United States of America

*McFarland & Company, Inc., Publishers
    Box 611, Jefferson, North Carolina 28640
    www.mcfarlandpub.com*

Contents

Contents

Contents

Contents

Contents

Contents

Introduction

Dear Poet,

Please let me introduce myself. I've been writing since I was eight years old, with an eleven-year writing pause between the ages of 24 and 35. I've attended writers' groups since I was a teenager. I've been reading, writing, critiquing, teaching, publishing and promoting poetry on a daily basis for decades.

I co-own and operate Accents Publishing, an independent literary press, where I've selected, edited and published more than a hundred poetry collections. Virtually all my friends are poets. I read poetry for fun as well as for work, although I enjoy it so much that I feel embarrassed to call it work.

Through practice, teaching and observation, I've accumulated a number of hard-earned practices in conceiving, arranging, editing, publishing and promoting poetry books. As an editor, publisher and mentor, I've carried a number of collections through all stages of completion, and I have found that certain processes and rules of thumb have helped every one of these books. This is not to say that the process is empirically predictable. I consider it very much an art, but it is possible to be guided step by step to satisfying results. I have found myself repeating these steps and applying certain philosophies so many times that I finally decided it's time to commit them to a craft book.

The Poet's Guide to Publishing invites you on a journey from being faced with a pile of poems to celebrating at your book launch. It's organized into five sections to mimic the five distinct phases in which I divide the process. To demystify and ground this work, each section provides a mix of theoretical materials and practical assignments.

I hope that this book (re)energizes you and, if needed, provides a lifeline throughout the process of turning your material into a well-edited, well-published and well-cared-for collection.

Here I'd like to share a few quirky details about me. In addition to having graduated with an MFA from the Naslund-Mann Graduate School of Writing, I have a background in computer science and project management as well as a degree in business administration. I apply a few of the best practices I've learned in these seemingly unrelated disciplines to the art of poetry. Art is science, science is art.

This guide is designed to meet you where you are in your book creation or publication process. It will be especially useful to those of you who have been writing for some time and have already accumulated a volume of work. Furthermore, it will be beneficial for you to belong to a writers' group, where you can workshop and get feedback on individual poems, and to have a few poet friends and colleagues willing to exchange manuscripts along the way.

Certainly, the process outlined in this guide is not the only way to stuff a porcupine, so to speak. I am sure that for every example or piece of advice between these covers, someone could come up with a brilliant counterexample or counter advice. What I've described here, however, has been my way of working with my own material and the approach I've given my students to work with theirs. As a friend once said, "Take what you like and leave the rest."

I've worked on this book for a number of years. During the past two, I created the Poetry Book Boot Camp—a five-month workshop that follows the material in this book. A few of the participants in these groups have agreed to share their experience with the tools and processes, and you'll read their stories and examples throughout the book.

PART 1

Concept

Projects

If you've read the introduction, you already know that I have a background in project management, software project management, to be more specific. Applying the principles of project management to writing and publishing books—my own or someone else's—has had a vital role in the success of bringing these books into existence.

I consider each poetry collection a project and treat it as such. If you're not doing this already, I'd love for you to adopt the idea that whenever you are beginning the journey from a pile of poems to a published volume, you are starting a project. What does this mean for you?

A project is a focused, planned and temporary set of activities. For a time, you focus your efforts and apply them according to a plan to reach a goal. What is the goal in this case? Since you're reading this guide, I assume your ultimate goal is to publish a poetry book.

Steve Jobs once said, "Real artists ship." You need to complete your project for it to count. In the appendix, I elaborate on several slippery rocks on the roadmap to completion. Many a book contains prescriptions of what to do. Many fewer discuss what *not* to do, maybe because there are almost infinite ways to quit. Disruptions, delays and restarts bring valuable insight but are also costly in terms of time and creative output.

To me, a book is not finished until it makes the leap from software into hardware—meaning, until it gets published. Publishing a book is a way of disconnecting from it, partly because you need to release control. This sentiment is even echoed in the term "book release."

The Three Aspects of Writing Poetry

I believe that there are three basic yet critical, unsubstitutable aspects to the process of writing poetry. These are instinct, technique and obsession.

Aspect One: Instinct

Instinct enables you to make good initial choices. The better instincts you have, the more you'll trust yourself to recognize when you've written something worth keeping. It helps you get oriented amidst a wide range of choices. Poets with underdeveloped instincts have difficulty making decisions about their work, separating good poems from not-so-great ones. Without the benefit of instinct, poets might be too susceptible to criticism and basically give up their own opinions in favor of someone else's. This is not to say that the author's opinion is always precious and impeccable, but the author is the only one aware of the reason for creating the work, and it's dangerous to shape a poetry book without a strong connection to this reason. I believe that instinct is sharpened by reading and listening to other people's work, consuming a wide range of diverse poetic forms, shapes and styles, and studying other literary genres. Instinct is essential for your poetry because it is unique only to you, and it is the basis of your poetic voice. To me, instinct is the unconscious part of writing.

Aspect Two: Technique

Technique is the skill necessary to actually execute, to complete the task of transforming the idea into language and shaping it in some representative way. It is the act of mirroring a specific type of energy into a specific outcome. Of course, in order to have strong technique, you need to practice. There is no substitute for actually writing in order to master the craft. If you have good instincts and poor technique, you may find that you like the idea of the work better than its manifestation on the page, and you might hear yourself saying something such as "this sounded better in my head." The sharpening of the technique is achieved by the dutiful practice of the craft. Normally it takes years, and not in the single digits, either. Have you noticed that often the most accomplished and admired poets are not in their twenties, and it takes decades for a poet to write their best work? I believe that in writing, age is an advantage, and to me, that is a comforting thought, because I hope to write for as long as I live. Technique is what enables us to edit our poems to the point we can call them finished. Technique, to me, is the conscious part of writing.

After instinct has served you to draft a poem, technique will help in making conscious decisions on each line break, internal/external rhyme or punctuation. In certain cases, technique overpowers the instinct, and that manifests as overediting. Again, stay connected to the reason for the poem; otherwise, you might edit it into something unrecognizable that is impeccable in technique but holds no energy for you. I call these "zombie" poems, poems that have been hollowed out of the reason for their existence.

Aspect Three: Obsession

My definition of obsession is "What do you think about when you don't have to think about anything?" The thoughts that go through your head on a regular basis have a much better chance of being put on paper. And then to be put on paper again. If you are obsessed with a subject/theme/person/poetic form, you have an opportunity to create a body of work relating to this subject. Each poem on a particular theme serves as a brushstroke of a painting or a facet of a crystal. Obsession is what lends energy to your writing, what interests you enough to write about. If you are not aware of your thoughts, here is an exercise: try to *not* think about anything and see what pops up. Futile attempts at meditation could be eye-opening too. If you don't know what you're obsessed with, or if you believe you are not obsessed with anything, ask people who know you well—they might give you valuable insight. Ask your spouse, parents, children. If you have people obsessed with you, it may be helpful to ask them. Remember that your obsessions do not have to be acceptable or interesting to others but should hold energy for you.

Why do you need an obsession? Obsession helps ensure that the writing happens. You could do many things with your time, and you make choices hour by hour. And if you do not find something stimulating enough—either positively or negatively—you won't write about it. (Unless it's a class assignment. Then you'll stop writing as soon as the class is over.) It feels good to write a poem, correct? The energy released in writing a poem alleviates the tension to some degree and provides more energy for writing other poems. If the obsession is complex and largely unexplored, there is a good chance you will write multiple poems on the same topic, even entire collections. I believe that an obsession has both conscious and unconscious elements, and the process of pulling the unconscious out into the conscious is what makes poetry a process of telling the truth about ourselves to ourselves.

Why is this important? While exploring obsessions, you are working in series, and this can give your book an excellent chance for interesting architecture. We will explore book structure and its elements in part two of this book.

Working in Series

Have you ever felt as though you were writing the same poem over and over? Have you ever had the urge to creatively explore a certain topic? Have you believed that *you in particular* have a unique perspective due to your life experiences, background, etc.? Such focus on producing poems clustered around a specific topic or theme I call writing in series.

At times the topics we tackle in our poetry are bigger than the individual poems. At times we write dozens of poems that seem to be related to one another and are, indeed, part of a story. At times we want to look at the larger theme from different angles, at different stages, or we want to talk to it with different voices.

I'll share a personal example. Last century I worked as a software engineer and a UNIX system administrator and always insisted that writing programs was akin to writing poems. You use language, syntax, form, intention. You have an audience—the computer, in this case. The fact that the programmer receives instant feedback is an added benefit—does the computer understand you or not, i.e., does the program run as intended? Furthermore, I observed that the commands used to administer the system resemble the workings of human society and mimic real-life concepts. As a bonus, the programming manual is titled *The Man Pages*. So, in my opinion, this concept is simply begging to be "coded" into poems. I've carried this obsession for decades, and over the years I've repeatedly failed in my attempts to write a series of poems.

In 2020, however, I decided that instead of writing poems about the commands, I could use the actual manual entries to create erasure poems, each based on a distinct UNIX command. I used the text of 30 commands from *The Man Pages* to create 30 erasures. A few titles of these poems (identical to the titles of the actual commands) were accept, bind, choke, clock, daemon, join, make, kill, last, touch, talk, test, trap, rename. The manual entry of each command explained the function, origin and use of this command, while the corresponding erasure poem attempted to distill the text into exposing a societal sore.

Indications of Successful Writing in Series

Successful writing in series propels your writing. The poems clearly belong together and inform, complement and strengthen each other. Often previous poems provide background for later ones. Within a manuscript not all work needs to stand alone, meaning you can place poems in context. This liberates you from the responsibility of providing background in every poem. Basically, you can rely on the reader to carry knowledge and attitude from earlier poems to later ones. It is reasonable to expect that the reader is experiencing the book from beginning to end, although that's not always the case, and you have no way of enforcing it.

When you're working on a themed manuscript, the reader can follow a narrative—beginning middle and end, although not necessarily in this order. The manuscript feels like a book, rather than a group of poems. How can you test this theory? If you add a random poem, it likely would seem out of place and raise the question "Why is this poem here?"

When writing in series is successful, in the process of working on the manuscript you may discover that you have more and more to say. If so, you may keep on generating related material. A welcome side effect might be that you are able to "upgrade" the manuscript by replacing old poems with new ones or simply add more pages to the collection. It may even turn out that you have more poems than you need, and that is a good problem to have, because at that point you can select only the best ones.

For my *Man Pages* collection of erasures, I was able to accumulate material with ease. The poems looked good together and had interesting form and similar tone—simultaneously abstract and impersonal, with an abundance of allegory and metaphor. A reader would immediately see kinship and interaction among the poems in the set.

Indications of Unsuccessful Writing in Series

The first and most obvious sign is not having enough poems. Anyone who has attempted an abecedarian chapbook but has barely written only three of the 26 coveted poems can relate to this experience.

Sometimes we think we have a lot to say on a theme, but it turns out we are unable to write about it or we simply dislike the result and find it unusable. Or maybe we need a different approach? Or maybe we're attempting the wrong genre? Maybe we're not ready yet? I'm continuously faced with examples of how much time it takes from getting the jolt of an idea to having actual material to work with.

Another sign that the writing in series is not quite working out is when the poems we produce feel repetitive in any or all aspects of form, language, content or tone. Then the resulting manuscript, or portions thereof, can become predictable and, sadly, boring. This happened to my *Man Pages* project. The poems were repetitive in form (erasure), language (sparse, prescriptive), content (computer commands and instructions) and tone (abstract with heavy reliance on metaphor). None of the components varied across the poems, so they became predictable. I got bored with my own work and decided that, unfortunately, this series of poems could not stand on its own. This was not a tragedy, however. I ended up using the best poems from this series in a supporting role for another project.

Maximizing the Chances for Success

Whenever writing in series, the most important question to ask yourself is "What else can I write about within this theme or on a related subject matter?"

Normally an answer follows, regardless of whether you're able—or willing—to follow up on it. Researching the larger topic typically answers this question and can even produce surprising results. This is very much searching for inspiration or, at least, making yourself wide open to it. I know poets who have scheduled research retreats and have done exhaustive due diligence in research in order to examine the material from all possible angles.

B. Elizabeth Beck, the author of *Painted Daydreams: Collection of Ekphrastic Poems*, did extensive research while working on her manuscript:

> Research enhances ekphrastic writing. Because a viewer can only glean so much information from gazing at a painting, a sculpture, or any other form of visual art, learning more about the artist can bring a poem to life. Specificity in verse is most effective for universal experience. As an art history teacher, I had an opportunity to research to write *Painted Daydreams: Collection of Ekphrastic Poems*. In Miro's painting, *Carnival of Harlequin*, there are many images to explore, yet while researching Miro's life, I learned he was so poor that one winter, he traded with a local farmer. This provided

an exciting opportunity to create the opening line of the poem, *Carnival of Harlequin DARE DREAM*, which states, "Your stomach full of radishes/sours breath belched in heart-/broken exhaustion." With that one specific detail, Miro springs to life as a living, breathing human, which enhances the poem.

Kandinisky's *Compositions* paintings are familiar to many, but does everyone know that his maid accidentally knocked over one of his paintings while he was out taking a walk, attempting to solve the problem of this composition? The relief he felt, "as you fall to/your knees and weep to see/your own painting on its side" is a bit of melodrama the poet imagines, but it is a detail I found researching that enhances the reader's experience beyond the poem merely explaining an abstract painting.

Collecting ideas in any way possible is a good practice. It may start by deliberately identifying what is missing from the manuscripts and attempting to fill in these holes. A kind, impartial reader can be invaluable at this stage, since the author is not always aware of what questions, confusions or curiosities a reader might have.

For example, for the *Man Pages* project I took the time to browse through the online Linux manuals, making lists of intriguing or provocatively sounding commands that I could potentially turn into erasure poems. I deliberately overachieved in generating a longish list, so whenever the time to work on an erasure poem opened up, I had the luxury of considering a number of commands to see which possibility excited me the most. This pre-work of deliberately listing the possibilities saved me time and helped me arrive in a creative space faster.

In my experience, it's generally helpful to produce more material than you need, so when you start selecting and arranging, you have the luxury of more to choose from.

Ultimately, though, if you need more poems, that means you also need more time.

Push and Pull Poems

I categorize most poems as "push" or "pull" poems.

Push poems are those that appear out of nowhere. You walk down the street, and a sentence or an expression appears in your head. You instantly recognize it as poetry. If you write that line down, immediately another one follows. Push poems produce seemingly effortless first drafts.

But how do you recognize if the thought in your head is poetry? I have two criteria:

(1) It surprises me. If the thought in my own head alerts me to something that I didn't know before or brings some new awareness to the forefront, I feel that I need to stop whatever I'm doing and listen. I have trained myself to write things down as soon as this delightful jolt of surprise appears.

(2) If you write the first line, more lines almost automatically follow, as if independent of you and your conscious awareness. The best way to describe this minor miracle is as an ocean current. Yes, the current is part of the ocean, but it has its own temperature, direction, speed.

A push poem pushes you, requests to be written. I consider push poems comparatively rare gifts, and I am grateful for every one that has made its way to me.

With **pull poems**, the author "pulls" from what's already available in their mind. The author goes in search of the poem, not the other way around. On such occasions there is no surprise—we know what we want to say and what our goal is. The author employs skill and technique to write a "well-made thing." Despite the lack of mystery surrounding pull poems, writing them is a nontrivial task. Exploring one's inner landscapes can give pull poems depth and beauty just as necessary as the spontaneous revelation of push poems.

Whenever we set out to fill the gaps in our themed manuscripts, we engage in writing pull poems. In the process, a few push poems may pop out as well. Most manuscripts contain both kinds of poems, and in the final result the reader should not be able to tell the difference.

Noticing Trends and Making Decisions

Learning to notice trends early yet making decisions as late as possible could be a valuable skill at this stage. For example, you see that you've written two daughter poems and one mother poem this week and still feel considerable energy around the topic of family. You've noticed a trend, so you can start contemplating where exploring such a trend may lead. A chapbook focusing on mother-daughter relationships? A set of poems to add to an already existing manuscript? Deliberately considering the "what else can I write about within this context" question might yield welcome writing assignments.

In short: You noticed a trend, dared to extrapolate where it might lead, and attempted to produce more related writing.

In my software development years, I learned about the value of making final decisions about your code as late as possible, and I see how this concept beautifully transfers to manuscript development. The writer needs to be aware of all options, since making decisions limits possibilities. This is not the time to narrow alternatives. At this stage, the poet needs to maintain awareness of what is possible. The decisions at every subsequent stage will keep narrowing the wiggle room of the manuscript until the final version has been reached.

Poetry Book Boot Camp participant Shelda Hale shares the following:

I taped the advice "See trends early, Make decisions later" to my computer monitor, because it was a powerful reminder for processing patterns of thinking. This practice let me consider poems that held promise and kept me from eliminating ones that became important in the final manuscript. For example, I started with a preconceived notion to organize poems on topics of my adult relationship to my parents. Allowing trends that did not meet that initial idea gave me more freedom to let the manuscript develop organically and to write new poems. I was able to reorganize and create a unified body of work that included poems about the complex relationships with my mother, father and myself at different stages of our lives. I keep that note on my computer to this day.

Gathering the Material

Regardless of how you've created your materials—push or pull poems, poems written over time or poems generated during the exploration of a theme—you need to consider what you have and how you might be able to use it in a potential collection.

Identify all poems you have not already published in a full-length book. Typically, you can reuse everything you've included in chapbooks, and poets often absorb some work from their previously published chapbooks into future full-length collections. A few pages later I will attempt to demystify the difference between chapbooks and full-length collections and to highlight the pros and cons of either choice.

If you are further along in your career and have had the heartbreaking experience of seeing your published books go out of print, why not add these poems to the consideration set too, especially if you are interested in creating a themed collection and "reusing" a few poems would help your case?

Print all poems you identified. I understand that printing a large number of pages could create inconvenience and even expense, but I believe that it's impossible to do this work effectively without having hard copies of everything. Physically handling paper gives you the ability to effortlessly shuffle sheets and to spread out the work for a better look.

Where to lay out the paper? Any flat surface is a candidate, of course. Beds, floors, tables ... the bigger the project, the larger the area it would require. This need for undisturbed space is a major argument for packing your papers and going on a private retreat for a few days, though I realize it's not always possible and certainly not every time you attempt to rearrange your poems. Thus, often you need to make the most of your living quarters. For manuscripts requiring longer-term consideration, you could even tape the poems to the walls. I am a fan of this option because it's largely pet- and child-proof. A hard-earned warning, though ... make sure you don't use permanent tape as it will damage your walls.

When you are ready to start working with the material, see if you can **read all the poems in one sitting** or at least in the same day. To make good decisions, you'll need be able to remember lots of text. A large set of considerations should be "uploaded" to your brain, and you will need to guard this mindspace from anything that might derail you. Set aside a solid stretch of time and avoid interruptions.

Poetry Book Boot Camp participant Bill Verble shares the following:

> I did sit and read through the poems I selected for the manuscripts. I probably did more skimming than a close reading, since some of the poems were in initial drafts but fit the theme that emerged from the poems I had written. Doing the reading in one day was helpful in confirming the thread running throughout the stack and validating that I had mostly selected the right ones. There were a handful I knew might be on the margin but I kept them after the first read.

Discovering Themes and Topics

As you are reading, **examine the poems**. Sometimes the themes and topics in one's poetry are obvious, at other times more subtle, but the process I'm describing is usable in either case.

Write simple labels on each poem or place sticky notes with keywords indicative of the theme on them. For example: family/birds/relationships/spiritual/political, etc. Tip: If you consistently write (or place) the labels at the upper right corner, it will be easier to thumb through and review these labels even after you've clipped the sheets together.

As you are labeling, **sort the poems**. Physically separate the poems into distinct stacks by themes and topics. This will help you see at a glance what topics predominate your material.

In reality, certain poems might belong to more than one pile. Whenever you encounter such a case, you can label the poem with both themes and place it in the stack corresponding to the poem's dominant theme or the stack for the theme you wrote down first. If you have a good number of multi-themed poems, you could gather them in a pile of their own. Identifying multi-themed poems is helpful because these intersections serve as links between themes.

For example, if you have a group of spiritual poems and a group of poems about food, you can place any intersectional, double-themed poems between the two topics to help with flow. The first draft of *The Invisible Arm of Peace* (a collection of poems by Khairi Hamdan that I selected and translated) I arranged purely by laying out the themes and their intersections. I felt exhausted, yet had an extra free hour and really wanted to complete the first draft of an ordered manuscript. So I arranged the poems just by reading the labels instead of considering the poems. I didn't walk away with a brilliant draft, but it was a step forward and certainly a better place to resume work the next day.

Poetry Book Boot Camp participant Tabitha Dial shared the following about her experience:

Using two folders that grew rather plump, I arranged my piles by alphabetical order. Each general subject had its own paper clip. When there were multiple labels, which was frequently the case, I chose the primary, overarching label. Both folders were happily filled in the end, and I enjoyed the process. The care it required, and the tangible results were fun.

Can't recommend this process enough! I looked forward to writing labels and making piles. It helped me recognize my longtime tendencies towards topics like music, Mom, and myths. It was both a monumental and cathartic experience. Much of it was done during my job as a high school substitute, where students usually work on their assignments at their laptops. The rest was done at home.

Though the task seemed daunting, I was determined to make our group proud and get the task done. I've taken myself seriously as a poet for a few decades and found work that dated back to 2005. My sense of personal accomplishment upon physically compiling all that poetry propelled me forward. It was quite satisfying to review my favorite pieces.

The result was a possible five separate manuscripts, with leftovers.

Assessing What You Have

The simplest and most concrete way of assessing the volume of content at your disposal is, of course, through counting. It can be eye opening to see how much material you have accumulated just by consistently exploring particular topics. Think in terms of pages of poetry, instead of the number of poems, as pages of poetry is the metric that matters, especially if you need to decide whether to work toward a chapbook or to shoot for a full-length book.

Review the contents of each stack. Identify aspects of the theme that are yet to be addressed.

Consider what else you could write to fully explore a particular theme.

Look for relationships between piles. The poems may seem unrelated yet could still interact in interesting and innovative ways.

Chapbooks or Full-Length Collections?

It's important to understand the difference between chapbooks and full-length poetry collections, as this will affect your choices for structuring the material.

The most important distinction is the size. Chapbooks are shorter books of poetry. Most frequently the number of pages hovers around 26, although I've seen chapbooks with page counts from the low teens to the upper thirties, even forties. A full-length poetry book typically is a minimum of 48 pages.

Here are several signals that a chapbook might be a more appropriate project than a full-length work for you at this time:

1. You have a stand-alone work of 20–30 pages of poetry. Of course, the biggest reason to publish a chapbook is having a chapbook-size manuscript. Because of their smaller size, it's easier to assemble themed, fascinating and cohesive manuscripts, and, in my experience, publishers love to see themed chapbooks. (Almost all Accents chapbooks are themed.) This doesn't mean that you could not or should not put together a theme-free manuscript, especially if it is representative of your best work.

2. You don't have immediate plans for a full-length collection. In the United States it is perfectly acceptable to publish a chapbook of poems and then reuse these same poems (part of

them or even all of them) at a future time in a full-length book. This makes the chapbook a safe way to publish, because the work is not *used up*, and you can publish it again. You can take risks—give a chance to a new publisher or even publish it yourself.

3. You are between books. If you recently published a full-length book, and you think it will be years before you release another, you may consider working on a chapbook in the meantime, something like a preview of what you're working on now and what your fans and friends can look forward to in a future volume.

4. You need a home for the orphans. That sounds worse than it actually is. Often when you finish a manuscript, for one reason or another, wonderful poems don't make it in. Sometimes you have enough of these good poems to make another book. Take a look at what you have. You may be surprised.

Now, let's talk about cases when it is better to hold off on publishing a chapbook and focus your efforts on a full-length book.

1. You have enough material for a chapbook, but you don't feel ready to let go of it yet. If this is the case, try to explore the reasons why. Maybe you do have more to say and would rather keep the work close to the chest until you're done letting it emerge. If you publish the chapbook knowing that you have more to say, that may detract energy (and time) from writing (and publishing) the rest of the poems.

2. You have an opportunity to publish a full-length collection. If you will be publishing a full-length book shortly thereafter, *and* it will use the same poems, that could be a marketing mishap. One of the books will suffer due to cannibalization, and that probably will be the chapbook. Likely you'll choose the full-length book over the chapbook to read from and to promote.

Chapbooks have some disadvantages over full-length books. They rarely get reviewed, and due to their lower price, they rarely get distributed widely. Also chapbooks are thin, and you can't fit writing on the spine, which makes them more difficult to locate among the books in your library. In general, the expectations for a chapbook and a full-length book are different, and sometimes small presses start as chapbook publishers.

Metafiles

Every book I work on has its own folder on my computer. In this folder I keep a minimum of three files. One file contains the current, most up-to-date text of the collection. In another file I've put aside poems that at a certain point have been in the manuscript but for whatever reason I've pulled out. As work on the book progresses, you will start accumulating an increasing number of manuscript revisions in that folder in order to keep organized and ensure handy access to these snapshots.

And the third mandatory file is titled something like "meta.doc."

The concept and the naming stem from my days administering UNIX networks. To install a new program, the administrator would download a software package, unzip it and immediately look up a file typically titled "metafile." In this file the admin could find information about the program: data such as versions, revisions, and bug fixes as well as installation instructions.

Your manuscript's meta file is a dedicated space where you can document the vision for your book. The point is to meticulously and deliberately preserve ideas and intentions as soon as they appear in your head. It might be a note for a minute change or plans for a major overhaul. It might be a potential title, a dedication, a name to add to the gratitude list on the acknowledgments page. Write it down, even if you feel (especially if you feel) that you could not possibly forget it.

My metafiles typically contain a few of the following:

- possible epigraphs
- ideas for existing poems to add
- ideas for poems to write
- ideas about ordering, organization and/or architecture
- a list of people to send the manuscript for feedback
- a list of people to request to blurb the book when the time comes
- ideas for a cover design
- a list of appropriate publishers or contests to submit the completed manuscript
- assignments to myself, such as:
  - ° remove XYZ poem
  - ° rewrite the last poem in first person
  - ° read ABC book for inspiration
  - ° merge poems D and E into one

I have found metafiles invaluable, and I treat them as an integral part of the process. I assign metafile creation and upkeep as mandatory homework to all students I work with at the book level. Having a dedicated space to channel one's vision for the future collection encourages dreaming, aiming high and taking one's own ideas seriously. Good things, y'all. Good things.

Poet Manuel Grimaldi reflects on his experience with metafiles and a few of the tools in this book while working on his manuscript *I Will Let You Down*:

> From day one of the boot camp, I constructed a file entitled *Project Metafile*, and built it into subsequent folders, month by month. Things like *what my friends think I'm obsessed about, epigraphs, inspirational pictures, the nascent concept for the collection after*

labelling the poems, all the arrangements of the collection, the bonding of pairs which focused the work and narrowed the choices, work assignments for myself in divorce humor (some that worked, some that didn't), book titles before the amazing book title exercise became known to us. Finally, looking at individual poems from a book view is a great boon of the metafile, because the basic notes are there. For example, *Take out poem x because poems y and z agree more harmoniously in its absence, and it may sing better in another place, or not at all.*

What is really helpful to me looking back on the first two months is how disorganized and overeager I was to get to the end, without taking stock of where I was. Taking breaths. Taking time. Reading. I learned how hard I *force* things to happen. When as my mother says in her Spanish *"tomatelo con calma, hijo"* (take it with calmness, son). Metafiles are tools to build a collection and a better poet. No joke.

Formally Listing the Possibilities

As important as anything else in the process of conceptualizing a poetry manuscript is to formally list the possibilities. What could be created out of this material that you've gathered, labeled, sorted, examined? My recommendation is to actually write out the possibilities in your metafile.

Once you have the possibilities, you will be able to decide where to start.

Illustration

Poet A enjoys writing about the natural world. Counting the sheets in the sorted stacks shows that she has 10 poems about land animals, 13 poems about birds, five poems about fish and 20 poems on seemingly random topics.

So what else could Poet A write about?

• What about mythical animals?
• What about pets?
• What about subterranean creatures? Fossils? Endangered, extinct animals?
• What about dreams about animals?
• What about Poet A's own animal nature?

I consider making an exhaustive list an act of due diligence.

At this point Poet A can formally list the possibilities. Looks like it might make sense to put together an animal-themed chapbook. If the goal is to have a full-length book, more work will need to be produced.

After Poet A has formally listed the possibilities, she will be able to examine them. Which possibility is the most exciting to this poet? Which one gives her body an influx of joyful energy and makes her mind buzz? That would be a good place to start.

A Corny Illustration

You are in possession of two sausage links, a cup of dried lentils, a gallon of milk, a pound of sugar and eight eggs. You place the ingredients on the counter to assess what kinds of foods you could create. You can combine these ingredients into a variety of meals.

Then you decide on the possibilities:

I could whip up an omelet.
I could go for a sausage and eggs dinner.
I could make lentil soup.
Or lentil soup with sausage.
I cannot make chocolate milk since I have no chocolate, but I can make crème caramel out of eggs, milk and sugar.

Then you determine which possibility you're most excited about. What do you feel like cooking?

In the same way you can arrange a number of books with your poems. Analogous to the cooking example, the ingredients are the piles you made earlier (for example, mother, father, cats, relationships, travel).

The list of possibilities are the different books that the *ingredients* could be shaped into (a chapbook about death of mother, full-length book about traveling with cats).

Then, you can choose a project. Needless to say, the book you decide to work on may not be the book you end up creating. Nothing is set in stone. Your decision at this point affects mainly the starting point and not as much the final collection.

Then, you need to start arranging the poems.

If You Cannot Find a Theme

It is rare to not notice at least one theme in a body of work, but if that's the case, you can adopt other strategies. You might be able to focus on forms, shapes, sizes or something else you find in common. You might be able to sort the work into stacks of haiku or sonnets, for example. Or piles of long poems or short poems, or prose poems and lyrical poems, or particular emotions present on the page.

Additionally—and especially if you're working on your first book—it's acceptable to adopt a more generic manuscript concept. For example, your goal could be to create a chapbook of your best poems written during the past X number of years. It's possible to have a well-ordered, well-structured book without a tight theme. And who knows? Once you get started, a theme might reveal itself in the process of working with the material.

Poet Linda Freudenberger shares the following experience:

During Poetry Book Boot Camp, it was daunting for me to create a manuscript of poems that could fit together. My poems dealt with grief after the loss of my husband, but then I began to see another theme emerge: Nature. There were poems about trees, dogs, tropical fish, that share my love for nature. These poems emerged into the second part of the manuscript. They were the beyond part of the manuscript manifesting signs of hope.

Qualities Needed at This Stage

Tolerance for ambiguity. You need to be able to sit with the uncomfortable feeling of lacking clarity. Allow yourself to not know what you are doing and trust the process. As a rule, the writing is smarter than the writer. It will make sense eventually.

Willingness to waste effort and time. There are no tears in baseball and no guarantees in poetry. In reality, no effort is wasted. Every attempt at the very least teaches you something about your own work and helps you discover the most suitable approach. The effect of these repeated efforts is highly cumulative, and you will be able to benefit from your work when starting subsequent projects.

PART 2

Arrangement

"If the path before you is clear, you're probably walking someone else's."—CARL JUNG

Combinations and Permutations

While the arranging of a manuscript is one of the most fascinating, creative challenges there is, a poet can easily get overwhelmed by the number of variations possible.

Statistically speaking, there is a massive set of possibilities and approaches. Let's take a moment to demonstrate just how massive it could be.

If you have a set of items to arrange in any order with no restrictions, you're working with combinations and permutations—in other words, being faced with a pile of poems before any decisions are made.

If you have 26 poems, the possibilities amount to this impossible number: 403,291,461,126,605,635,584,000,000. I don't even know what this number is, although I wouldn't mind winning that many dollars in the lottery.

If you have 26 poems and you decide on the first and the last one of the collection, then the number of possibilities shrinks to "merely" 620,448,401,733,239,439,360,000.

If you are working with 13 poems, the possible combinations would be 39,916,800 after selecting the beginning and the ending poems.

I've included these statistical examples to demonstrate that once we start making decisions, the possibilities drastically diminish.

Reducing the Number of Combinations with Bonded Pairs

Those of you who have owned pet ferrets know that ferrets are often sold two at a time. That's because when they get attached to one another, they start doing everything together. They sleep snuggled together, drink water together, play together. The pet shop employees call them a "bonded pair" and sell both or neither. (Admittedly, it could be a sales trick, though I was happy to succumb.)

I got the idea of bonded pairs in poetry when I noticed that certain poems seemed to stick together, no matter how much I rearranged the rest of the manuscript. So regardless of how many combinations existed in the manuscript, these two poems were "glued" to one another. I considered them a bonded pair and treated them as a single poem. Then I tried to match as many bonded pairs as I could within the set of poems I was facing. Once I bonded a pair, I would start moving that pair from place to place as a unit. Both poems or neither.

Thus, if you start with 26 poems and decide on 13 bonded pairs, in reality you're effectively working with only 13 poems. Thirteen is much easier to arrange than 26.

Such a distributed approach reduces the pressure of starting at the beginning and building a manuscript to the end. As I said before, many poets feel overwhelmed because they don't know how to start. In other words, by using the concept of bonded pairs, you can make significant progress on your manuscript without having a clear idea of what you're doing.

Strive to find as many bonded pairs as you are able. Some of the pairs might actually turn out to be trios, even quartets, which would further speed up the process.

Then you can try to bond some of the bonded pairs and fuse them into bigger chunks. Every time you make a choice about placement or bonding, you're reducing the possibilities.

Notice that the narrowing of possibilities is the general trend of all activities after you formally list the types of collections you could possibly create out of your poems—from a wide range of possibilities, to a narrowing set of choices that feel right to you thematically and aesthetically.

How to Bond Poems

I believe that many poets intuitively know how to do this already. Most poems naturally stick together thematically. One of the poems may ask a question, and the other could answer it. One may describe an action, and the other may continue this action. One may make a statement, and the other may serve as a commentary. One of the poems may prove a point, and the other may contradict it, since contrast also could be a bonding factor.

Poet Marianne Peel shares her experience:

I find the organizational technique of "bonded pairs" to be especially useful when organizing a poetry manuscript. Working on a collection that chronicled the lives of five generations of the feminine divine in my family, I intuitively organized the manuscript in a linear fashion: my grandmother, my mother, myself, my four daughters, and my granddaughter. Although this linear organization worked, the order of the poems seemed stiff and somewhat predictable. At the suggestion of an editor, I was charged with reorganizing the manuscript in a nonlinear way, letting the poems speak to one another across several generations. Instead of a collection of poems about the females in my family over the generations, the manuscript evolved into a collection that focuses on the movement from innocence to experience.

Though it seemed a daunting task at first, I was immediately freed from my paralyzing fear by starting with a technique that is highly manageable: bonded pairs. I literally mixed up the pages of the manuscript, tossed them onto the floor, and then searched for bonded pairs ... poems that talked to one another in ways that I had not considered initially. What this did for the manuscript was nothing short of magical. Images, themes, motifs, etc. began to show themselves to me in ways I hadn't seen before. As a result, the manuscript is more creative, free of go-to conventions like linearity, and filled with surprises that hopefully keep the reader engaged from poem to poem.

For example, I paired *I Begged My Mother for a Doll* with *Barbie and I Share the Same Birth Year: 1959.* Initially, these two poems were in two very different sections of the manuscript. As I considered the guiding principle of bonded pairs, I determined these two poems should be next to one another. The first speaks from a young child's point of view, jealous of the doll of the neighbor girl across the street. The second poem delves into deeper ramifications associated with images the media/manufacturers give us about identity, body shape and size, what constitutes beauty, etc. What I ended up realizing is that these two poems truly speak to one another, illuminate one another, in ways having them in separate parts of the manuscript failed to do.

Themeless Manuscripts

Let's consider the case where you have not been able to find a tight theme for your poetry collection and you'd like to make the most of the best work you have. Here is an outline for a possible process.

You would still start with a printout of all your poems and try to read them in one sitting. However, you'd sort each poem into one of the following three stacks:

Best poems. In it put your best work, the poems you cannot imagine the manuscript without, the poems you definitely want to include. This set will be the main source of material for your manuscript, its core.

Back to the drawer. This pile will contain unfinished or simply not-good-enough poems as well as the occasional I-wrote-this-just-for-me-and-don't-want-to-share. Likely none of these poems will make it into the book.

Maybe. These are poems that may or may not work in the collection. They may look good under certain conditions, in a supporting role, or if the manuscript shifts towards a theme. And sometimes poets just flip-flop on certain texts and alternate between including them and pulling them out. Those long-suffering poems belong in the maybe stack.

After sorting the piles, put the "Back to the drawer" stack back in the drawer, slide the maybes aside and start with the best poems. You may then select the first and last poems and arrange the remaining material in an order that makes sense to you. Examine the resulting manuscript to determine if you want to add anything from the "Maybe" pile. Take a snapshot, arrange it into an editable document on your computer and take a break.

Repeat as many times as necessary.

The Iterative Approach

In a past life, I worked as a project manager for high-tech, high-risk software projects. There we employed the iterative approach as the only sane way to build, test and release on time, while not creating a big, unmanageable mess.

Under the paradigm of the iterative approach, the desired functionality of a larger project evolves from the buildup of smaller, distinct deliverables (aka iterations), each constituting an improvement upon the previous version. Each iteration is enhanced by adding features or upgrading quality. This way of thinking and working translates well to our work here, I promise. A second, expanded edition of the book you're reading could be considered another iteration. A chapbook is a prior iteration of a full-length collection, as are the various drafts along the way and in between.

You can benefit by utilizing the iterative approach while developing your manuscript from first draft to full release. You do not have to fix all bugs at once. You don't have to improve, edit, or polish everything right away. You only need to implement incremental improvements upon a previous version.

Poetry Book Boot Camp participant Renee Rigdon shares the following:

> I tried to never make too many changes in one sitting. Changing too many pieces at once is sort of like adding seasonings to a pot of soup without tasting it to see what it needs. I tried to add, change, or remove only one or two elements at a time, then let the book rest for the remainder of the day. There were definitely times when I would make overarching changes to the entire manuscript all at once, caught up in the flow, which was sometimes the right answer.

In order to successfully employ the iterative approach in manuscript development, it's important to adopt a suitable rhythm of revision, snapshot and rest. The rhythm is individual to the poet's temperament and schedule. Similarly, the improvement over the previous draft could vary from negligible to revolutionary based on energy level, availability and inspiration. Meanwhile, the folder with your project accumulates an increasing number of files, each a snapshot of the manuscript's best version at a particular date.

Snapshots

Let me state the obvious that there is no wrong way to arrange a poetry collection. That said, there is no right way, either. It's a highly subjective, very much trial-and-error process, and it's helpful to keep an open mind. Persistence is not always the best policy in book arrangement. Flexibility will prove more valuable, listening, updating, upgrading along the manuscript's evolution.

I recommend that every time you feel you've made progress—that you've made good decisions you don't want to lose—take snapshots. A snapshot provides a sort of backup. It gives you peace of mind, a safety net, so if a subsequent revision seems like a step backward, you could swiftly revert to a previous version. Furthermore, taking regular snapshots releases you from the obligation to remember the good combinations and could provide you with a sense of safety—you have something valuable, and you've managed to document it. Interestingly enough, revisiting the snapshots could reveal your process, thinking, the evolution (or the lack thereof) of various versions and manifestations of the collection. As a rule of thumb, if you feel you've achieved an ordering that you don't want to forget, it might be time to take a snapshot.

One way to do it is to literally photograph the poems in their arrangement on the couch, or on the floor, or wherever they happen to be laid out. One advantage of the photo approach is its speed and efficiency, and in most cases a few pictures are sufficient, especially if you haven't been able to arrange the entire manuscript but only a portion of it. It's worth taking a photo of a particularly successful poem sequence.

If you have a scanner handy, you can also scan the arranged manuscript into a pdf and email it to yourself for extra backup. Then you can store the snapshot in your project's folder, for example, "Spring Garden Feb 29 2023.pdf" or "Family Issues Manuscript June 10.pdf." If you have access to a multifunctional printer, all you'd need to do is place the stack of paper on the feeder, provide an email address, and the printer's workflow should take care of the rest. Two more advantages of scanning: (1) all poems are contained in the same file and (2) any notes you might have written on the pages are captured as well.

Poetry Book Boot Camp participant Renee Rigdon took snapshots the following way:

> I took snapshots of my manuscript by listing the current table of contents in my metafile with the date that it was recorded. I use toggle lists so that I can collapse older snapshots and reference them as I wish.

If you feel that you have a good-enough-for-now arrangement or that you won't be able to spend time with the manuscript for a while (either because your schedule precludes it or you simply need to step away for a break), you may want to follow up on the computer so that you have a file in an editable format that mirrors your arranged stack of poems. If time is at a premium, you could list just the titles in their latest order, though I recommend building a complete manuscript and pasting the actual poems as well. In that way, whenever you are able to resume work on your book, you can print a fresh, ordered representation of your best effort to date.

Upon accomplishing this, you have captured not only a snapshot but also a revision. You have completed a draft and made a (potentially major) step toward your goal. Please allow yourself to feel good, even if you fully realize the manuscript needs more work. It's time to feel like a hero and this also might be a good point to rest.

Taking a Break

After a complete revision it might be a good idea to step back from the manuscript for a time. It is not uncommon to need a break at this point. Immersing oneself in one's writing can be exhausting emotional work, so a restorative pause may help prevent you from burning out, numbing out or getting overwhelmed. Try resting *after* completing a revision, because such a milestone is likely accompanied by a sense of accomplishment, so you would be pausing on a high note with a boost of confidence. You have proof that you actually *can* do it! And if you're able to do it once, you can do it again.

Furthermore, I've noticed that whenever I'm focused on a manuscript and actively pouring energy into the work, I have no strength—or even desire—to do anything else, even if I have the time. So, if you are like me, taking a break to catch up on day-to-day life helps with … day-to-day life.

How long of a break? Any time from several days to several months. Whatever best matches your temperament and schedule.

Poetry Book Boot Camp participant Amy Richardson shares the following:

> I did take breaks. Sometimes, they were short. Walks or stretching between bouts of working on piecing together my poems into a whole manuscript. These allowed moments of pause during frustration, which often helped me come back after 15–20 minutes with a resolution for the issue at hand or a new idea about how I wanted to proceed with my poems. Other times, I took longer pauses. I would put everything away for a day or two (once an entire week) and allow my mind to focus on something else. This was especially helpful when my brain felt overloaded, and I seemed to be doing more harm than good for my manuscript while I tried to work. It also allowed my thoughts space to settle, so I came back to my document fresh and able to view it from a different perspective. I believe both types of breaks benefited in clearing my head and sharpening my focus. To separate myself from the work and to view it as a reader as opposed to clinging to parts that weren't working simply because I liked them.

In working on my own poetry books, I try to maintain a weekly rhythm for as long as I have a backlog of specific ideas for next steps and manuscript to-dos. In that way I harness the energy of enthusiasm to remain connected to the manuscript while continuing with daily life and other obligations. After following up on every improvement I can think of, I take a longer break to gain perspective. If I feel ready to hear feedback, I swap manuscripts with a poet friend who has work in a similar stage.

To avoid letting the process take forever, it is a good idea to commit to a deadline. I like to use submission dates for revision deadlines. Then I submit a particular revision to a particular opportunity.

Goes Without Saying, but ...

The baseline (first revision) doesn't have to be brilliant, coherent, or anything close to a final version. It needs to exist, functioning as a steppingstone. Also, the first draft (or any draft, for that matter) should not be "sacred," meaning, you should consider it to be changeable.

Once, in one of my poetry manuscript classes, I was giving instructions to the group along with the assignment of arranging a manuscript draft by our next meeting. Uncomfortable silence set upon the room.

"You can do it," I assured them.

The silence continued.

"You don't believe me, do you?" I continued pressing.

I got a few nods at that point. They didn't believe that they could.

"OK, then. Do you believe that by next week you can produce a poorly-arranged manuscript?"

That, they believed.

"OK, great! Next week's homework is to create a poorly-arranged manuscript."

And they did. Everyone who was brave enough to attempt the exercise was able to come up with an arrangement.

The following week's homework was to create a second draft.

Avoiding Distractions and More

At this stage it's best to keep your focus high-level and manuscript-wide and not get overly concerned with the fine-tuning and micro-editing of the individual poems. You will have an opportunity to do this in the following stage. Besides, it will save you time to only polish the poems that do make it in the manuscript and at this point you may not have a clear idea. Basically, you need the confidence that you will be able to "finish" those poem drafts after the manuscript is arranged. It might be beneficial to keep a list of to-dos and revision ideas that you plan to follow up on at the next stage. You already have a perfect destination for this kind of information—your project's metafile!

Poetry Book Boot Camp participant Wendy Jett shares the following:

> Getting all the poems together with just a first or second draft of each poem, then going back and editing/tweaking really worked for me. It helped me get the "big picture" of the manuscript and I think that allowed me to know how to edit to better fit the flow and feeling of the manuscript.

Poetry Book Boot Camp participant Bill Verble had the following to say:

> I had poems in rough form that I was editing while working on the arrangement of the manuscript. The first arrangement came together pretty quickly, and I was happy with it as a start. I then left the manuscript as it was and focused on editing individual poems. Many of the poems were initial drafts and needed revision, but I found it

---

helpful to revise in the context of other poems in the manuscript. One group of poems all started as individual works, but as I assembled the arrangement I saw a series emerge. I then began to revise them within the context of the series and how they would support one another. It was not until I completed a few rounds of editing poems that I went back and revisited the arrangement of the manuscript.

As I mentioned before, during the book arrangement process, the need to write more at a particular place becomes clear. (Example: "Wouldn't it be wonderful if I had a poem about my cat also, not only about my dog?") Sometimes poets are able to generate this material and sometimes they are not, or at least not yet. If the latter is your case, you may need to adjust the project or refocus it so that the lack you identified is not a detriment. To use the cooking example, if you have only one egg, you won't make an omelet, but rather boil it and chop it to top a salad.

And at times we simply do not know what to do next with the manuscript. We have taken it as far as we are able, we acknowledge deficiencies, we identify less-than-stellar aspects, but still we don't know how to proceed. I see three steps that might help in this situation: feedback from a trusted reader, a longer break from the manuscript, or reading more poetry books for inspiration and edification.

Book Organization

Poetry chapbooks, due to their smaller size, are normally organized in one long section. This is not to say that you cannot or should not section a chapbook, but I rarely see them divided. Often a chapbook, short for a "chapter book," could be viewed as precisely that—a section from a larger book—so it's already monolithic by its concept. Additionally, again due to size, it's easier to focus the content into a single tight topic, if your work coalesces around a theme. For example, the chapbook *Kings of the Rock and Roll Hot Shop, or What Breaks* by Lynnell Edwards explores the creative process of glassblowing. Jay McCoy's chapbook *The Occupation* gives the reader a glimpse of the speaker's life as an HIV-positive person.

Authors of full-length poetry manuscripts have the opportunity to experiment and zero in on interesting book architecture that supports the themes featured in the collection. Normally it takes quite a few iterations to arrive at the structure that would best cradle the content. Every attempt sets the stage for the next set of creative instructions that we await from the ether or from a colleague or a mentor.

In other words, most of the time the poet works in the dark, waiting for clarity, and that could be a seriously uncomfortable feeling, especially for those of us who need to feel in control. At this point many people give up, or effectively give up by stretching the process in time indefinitely.

In project management school we were taught that it is not possible to plan a trip so that all traffic lights would be green. In arranging a manuscript, we need to proceed one green light at a time. Multiple times. How many? We'll discuss this in the editing section.

Titles

Even before your book is judged by its cover, it will be judged by its title.

Most often the title of a poetry collection is derived from a poem inside that book—a poem title, or a line, or an expression. Rarely are the words not physically present in the collection. And even then, the author might say something like "The title comes from a poem that used to be part of the manuscript." Sometimes working titles end up as the final title because nothing better comes along. Sometimes the title arrives at the last moment, and in rare cases the title appears first—before any of the poems are written—as a harbinger of the future book.

A few examples of great Accents book titles:

Killer Poems by Andrew Merton
Available Light by Audrey Rooney
It's Not Easy Being a Moth by Mark Lee Webb
Fading into Bolivia by Richard Taylor
A Brief, Natural History of an American Girl by Sarah Freligh

The title of a collection performs a different function from the title of an individual poem. The book title needs to stretch as an umbrella above more than one poem; it needs to cover in some way the entire collection. What makes a good book title? One that is not a cliché, one that is memorable, broad, open to multiple interpretations.

Also one that is non-alienating. There are books whose titles you see and immediately think, "This is not for me" or "I don't want to read this." Sometimes there are cultural differences and titles do not carry over well from one language (or country) to another. I have an unfortunate example from my own biography. I published a book in Bulgarian, *How God Punishes*, and it was very well received. In a largely atheist country, such a title raised curiosity. When I published the book in English, however, interest in the book turned out to be minimal. It may have been a truly terrible book, but I like to think that the title played a role in the book's invisibility. In the United States, many people have unshakable views and relationships with God and are uninterested in other people's interpretations. The irony is that the book is not about punishment from God but instead discusses ego and self-sabotage.

Choosing a good title for your book is important because this title will become a permanent part of your bio, not to mention your life. I suggest keeping a list of possible book titles in your metafile and consider any title before publication a working title only, i.e., temporary and changeable. It is not uncommon for a manuscript to be accepted under one title and published under another.

By now you might have gathered several possible titles in your metafile. You may even have found "the one." Nonetheless, I'd like for you to go through the following title-hunting exercise.

Ideally, you'd come to this work rested, returning to your manuscript with fresh eyes after a break. Set the intention that you'll be "reading for titles." Then start from the beginning and circle (or underline) all potential titles you encounter in the text, all the way through to the last poem. Be methodical. You can think of yourself as a hunter of interesting phrases and intriguing poem titles that could represent your poetry collection. Aim for 15–20 minimum. List them all in a column. Then start shrinking the list until you have just two or three good candidates. The rest of the potential book titles could be used as section titles, and it's especially satisfying if you are able to select a set of titles that interact with one another in a symphony of titles.

I find Excel helpful during this process. I've included an example of my own title exercise when I was translating a book of selected poems by Palestinian-Bulgarian poet Khairi Hamdan. I started with 21 potential titles and many of them were easy to dismiss. Then I chose what I considered to be the best five and shared three of them with the author to get his feedback. My favorite was *Essence of Desert*, reflective of the images of Bedouins, camels and sand appearing in many of the poems. The author did not want this title, however, because he already had published other books with titles referring to sand and desert. He liked *The Invisible Arm of Peace*—because it underscores the spiritual thread consistent throughout all his work.

Initial Set of Potential Titles	Narrowed Set	Favorites	Offered to Author
handfuls of sand	handfuls of sand	reeling the universe	reeling the universe
whirling in the right direction	whirling in the right direction	the philosophy of survival	the invisible arm of peace
reeling the universe	reeling the universe	the invisible arm of peace	essence of desert
traces of grass	time of rest and absence	essence of desert	
time of rest and absence	residual fragments of exile	the hum of the universe	
residual fragments of exile	attempt for a leap in place		
I speak of you and me	petrified tenderness		
attempt for a leap in place	The Wisdom of the Iceberg		
Suffering Suits the Human Race	the waters of a wandering iceberg		
petrified tenderness	Survival Training		
The Wisdom of the Iceberg	the philosophy of survival		
the waters of a wandering iceberg	the invisible arm of peace		
Survival Training	essence of desert		
the philosophy of survival	the hum of the universe		
the invisible arm of peace	paths towards the outer world		
essence of desert			
between roar and peace			
at the edge of promise			
the hum of the universe			
paths towards the outer world			
the hum of the universe			

Poetry Book Boot Camp participant Amy Richardson has this to say about her experience with the title exercise:

I loved the title exercise. Titles are often the most difficult part of writing for me, so having a way to find one without just pulling the title of a poem within my manuscript or trying to come up with something entirely new was a wonderful experience. The process of combing through my document to look for lines that may work as potential titles also forced me to look at my poems in a different way and to think about them not just individually, but also as a piece of this whole I was creating. It was interesting to see the lines I highlighted and to list them in their own document as I considered them and the impact choosing one of them would ultimately have on my completed manuscript. It helped highlight the themes and places where my manuscript was cohesive, but also showed me some places and poems that weren't working the way I needed them to. Ultimately, my title became *Constellations on the Hillsides* because the imagery worked well with the themes throughout the manuscript.

One final, often sobering step of the process should be googling your potential book title or searching for it on Amazon. If you see several other books sporting the same title, you may have to move down the list to your next choice.

Titling a manuscript could be one of the most fun and celebratory parts of the process. Yes, it's intimidating, but also if you're choosing a title, that means you have a book. And *that* I find exhilarating every time.

Dedications

Think of book dedications as you would think of tattoos. Many seemed like a good idea at the time.

A couple of examples: (1) A friend of mine published a novel with a dedication to her husband, whom she divorced the following year. (2) Out of all books I've authored, I have only one with a dedication, and I honestly regret doing that. The person to whom

I dedicated the book and I had a falling out mere months after publication.

Most Accents books dedications have been added at the last minute. I would literally receive an email: "Is it too late to add a dedication?"

During my tenure as a project manager, I learned that as a rule, the features added at the last moment are the ones the customer will be the least satisfied with. This applies to last-minute changes.

I'm not trying to discourage anyone from adding a dedication; I'm saying that you don't have to. Do it only if you feel strongly and if the work calls for it. Think back to the classics. The more time goes by, the less important it is to whom the work has been dedicated.

Trigger Warning

Poet Melva Sue Priddy included a trigger warning at the beginning of her book *The Tillable Land*. When I asked her for her reasons, she explained that she wanted to protect herself as well as others. She wanted the potential readers to be aware of the types of traumatic stories inside so that they could make an informed decision whether to read the poems or not.

This is not a long-standing practice, though I think it might be here to stay. My opinion now is that it cannot hurt to have a word of caution, and it is a fair warning and a compassionate consideration for readers with PTSD. That said, the decision to include or to omit a trigger warning can be deferred to later stages of the publishing process and you can discuss it with your editor and publisher.

Table of Contents

Once, in the distant 2010, at a reading in Lexington, Kentucky, poet Jim Lally, the author of *Stick Tight Man*, got up on stage with my newly released chapbook and said, "Now I'll read you Katerina's book." Then he proceeded to recite the table of contents (TOC), line by line, with the intonation, pauses and diction reserved for reading poetry.

It was a fascinating experience for me because it taught me two things I hadn't considered until then.

1. The table of contents of a poetry book could function as a poem. In a very real sense, it *is* the very first poem of the collection.
2. Yes, you can read the entire book in the TOC.

Certain poetry collections feature leading poems, brought out in front of all sections. I'd argue that every collection with a table of contents at the beginning of the book already has such a poem.

Keep in mind that not every country has the practice of putting the table of contents in front, so be mindful of the geographical audience for your book. Additionally, certain collections forego the table of contents: books of haiku, or books where the book *is* one long poem or can be considered as such.

For example, A. Molotkov's *Your Life as It Is* is a chapbook of 21 poems where none of the poems has titles and every poem starts with the same line: "You wake up in the morning." A table of contents in this collection would serve no purpose and would be disorienting, at best.

Considering your own manuscript, go ahead and read through your table of contents, then try to answer these questions:

What does the table of contents say about my work?
What kind of expectations does it set?
What themes are brought to the surface?

If you do not yet have a manuscript, it might be fun to grab an unfamiliar poetry collection and read through the TOC to see what you can surmise about the book just from it. In the next section we will revisit the fine-tuning of the TOC and give examples of especially successful sequences.

Sections

One recurring question is whether to section the book or leave the poems in one longer, uninterrupted flow. My answer, in the form of a question, is "What does your poetry need?"

The beginning of a section indicates the start of an exploration of something such as an event, a period of time, an emotional state, a relationship, an attitude, etc. The end of a section often marks the completion of this event or time period or the end of our exploration of this matter. A subsequent section can pick up the thread at a different place or focus on a separate aspect or zoom in to a related issue.

For example, *Lock Her Up* by Tina Parker is a poetry collection about three women committed to a mental institution. She has structured the book in three sections—admission, treatment, and release—to mimic the process of the issue she's exploring. The sections as well as their titles succeed on both concrete and metaphorical levels. I asked Tina to walk us through the stages of her decisions and the evolution of her manuscript:

> Before *Lock Her Up* was a book, it was three file folders. Each folder held poems that focused on three character types: daughter, mother, and widow. My research into 19th and 20th century patient records of the Southwestern Lunatic Asylum revealed a pattern of fathers committing their daughters, husbands committing their wives, and adult sons committing their mothers. I developed composite characters to tell the stories of these forgotten women, and I initially thought the character types would organize the collection, with each character having its own section. This draft structure helped me to identify gaps and create new poems. However, the overall feel was too linear, too organized, and too simple. There needed to be more

mystery, as the patient records are themselves elusive and fragmented.

I experimented with three sections to represent 24 hours in the asylum: Morning, Noon, and Night. This was getting closer to a structure with the overall feel I was going for—it required interweaving the characters' stories, which is more effective than separating them. However, the final structure arose from pulling back even further and leaning into the "steps" we hear often in the medical field: Admission, Treatment, and Release. These section titles are cold and technical, which creates tension with the raw emotion of these untold stories.

I have come across books organized in sections where I've felt puzzled about the reasoning behind the separation. I've also read books where the "chapters" brilliantly underscored the book's development. I believe that it's generally a good idea to have some thematic link between sections; otherwise, it could feel like several unrelated chapbooks have been printed in the same volume. Also, I've noticed that if a book has one clear, single, dominant theme, it rarely yields well to sectioning.

Poetry Book Boot Camp participant Kathleen Gregg shares her experience:

At first, I organized my manuscript, *Love in Absentia*, into sections: my son meeting his bride-to-be in NYC, then moving to China; me and my husband traveling to China; Nate and Kitty coming home for a visit. I began each section with a Chinese proverb or a segment of Chinese poetry or a Chinese quote. But I wasn't happy with how much bigger the middle section was, compared to the other two. I decided to include more Chinese proverbs, quotes, poems in between smaller groups of my poems as a way to break up the manuscript without actually having sections. I feel like this strategy works really well. And the Chinese proverbs, quotes, poems add interest and relevance to the collection.

"Sections give the reader a break," said a poet once.

I wouldn't section a book to take it easy on the reader. I don't think that poetry needs to caretake the audience too much. Reading poetry is an energy-consuming and risky endeavor. The reader risks empathy, emotional involvement, attention to metaphor and excavation of meaning. Not everyone is ready or interested in investing such an effort, but those who regularly read poetry do so readily.

Masked Man, Black by Frank X Walker is a full-length book written and published in the fateful year 2020. It is a raw and timely recount of the pandemic lockdown and the murder of George Floyd. The poems in this collection pack the immediacy and gravity of letters from the trenches of a war. Frank arranged the book in one long sequence sans sections. This organization mimics the nonstop onslaught of news, issues and tragedies during the addressed time period.

In poetry, and generally in art, there is no "one size fits all" prescription, and this applies to the size of the sections. I don't feel that the sections need to be equal in size or a certain number. Among my own full-length collections, I have two books in three sections, one book divided into four, one divided into seven sections plus an epilogue, and two without any sections at all.

That said, if I decide to employ sections, I enjoy crafting section titles and epigraphs. In the metafile I likely have built a list of potential titles, and I itch for a chance to use more than one good title. I also try to ensure that all these titles interact with each other and also refer back the overall book title. Is this effort overkill or a good time? Yes.

I want to include a comprehensive example of an experienced poet's dance with her manuscript's structure. Libby Falk Jones has three previous poetry collections and at the time of this writing is working on another, titled *Southern Ladyspeak*. She described her trial-and-error attempts to find an optimal arrangement of her poems as well as going back and forth on the decision to use sections or not. The complete recount of her experience can be found in the appendix. Here I'm posting the portion where she shares the step that helped her get unstuck—the bottom-up approach of bonded pairs. In Libby's own words:

> My solution? Let go of structuring into sections and work instead on creating resonance between small sets of poems, pairs and triplets, while maintaining a rough time sequence, with poems drawing on childhood coming earlier, those focusing on marriage and motherhood coming later. In creating pairings and triplets, I looked for common subjects or approaches and also tried for variety in form and tone. Reading through the first rough order I created, I was able to fine-tune placement, moving a few poems a place or two. It was freeing not to have to think about the rationale for and coherence of a section, and instead to concentrate on the reader's experience of a couple or three pages. From one pair/triplet to the next, there was a gradual progression. I thought the experience of reading would be like stepping on one stone, hesitating, then stepping on another. There was a path, a beginning and an ending, through this world of Southern females. Katerina suggested paying particular attention to the relationship between the first and last poems in a collection. I was pleased with this pairing: the first poem brought an adult perspective to one experience in childhood, and last poem returned the adult speaker again to childhood, but with a focus on the experience of writing poems about the past.

Epigraphs

In the metafile for your project, it's a good idea to accumulate epigraphs that relate to the themes within the manuscript. There is no real downside to collecting more than you need. The worst that can happen is that you don't use them for this project.

Train your ear to catch usable phrases. Harvest epigraphs from anywhere, not only as you read poetry books but also from unrelated conversations.

Once, in 2010, in front of Natasha's Café in Lexington, Kentucky, I shared a moment with a gentleman down on his luck who was asking for spare change. I gave him a bit of cash and then we started talking. He said, "I've done some bad things," and I answered, "That might be so, but I still think you are a good man." My words took him by surprise, and he started crying and then said, "Promise me that I am good." I wrote down his words because I knew that I could use them somewhere. In fact, "Promise me that I am good" was an epigraph to an early version of my book *Second Skin*.

I heard my mentor Kathleen Driskell say that she writes her own epigraphs, and I liked the idea. I've used this practice in two of my own books as well. Do you have wonderful quips and one-liners that you have not been able to use in poems but could use as epigraphs? It's worth taking a look!

Poetry Book Boot Camp participant Joanie DiMartino had the following to share about her work with epigraph considerations while working on her manuscript *Wood to Skin*, a collection about the 19th-century whaling industry:

I was selected as a "38th Voyager" on the *Charles W. Morgan* in 2014. That summer, Mystic Seaport Museum sailed the *Charles W. Morgan*, which is the only wooden whaleship left in existence, up the New England coast for research on what was deemed the "38th Voyage." The *Charles W. Morgan* sailed 37 voyages as an actual whaler previously, before being decommissioned and becoming a museum artifact.

I began researching the historical documents to discover the realities of life on board a whaler, and also to seek out the poetry within a culture that no longer exists. All whalers were required to keep a daily logbook of each voyage, most often—but not always—a task assigned to the first mate. Voyages could last between three to five years, so in a complete logbook there is plenty of material to assess. Logbooks often simply detailed tasks and weather conditions in a brief shorthand, such as this one taken from the *Charles W. Morgan's* first voyage, dated Monday, September 13, 1841: "Comes with light breezes from the N and pleasant weather Watch Employed in Ships Duty Middle and Last part the same. Heading E." Latitude and Longitude were often attached. From a human interest perspective they can be a tedious read, with little beyond weather, navigation, and crew tasks. However, at times, unusual or necessary-to-document events were also written down, and these entries provided excerpts I was able to use as epigraphs to set the context for the poems that followed, such as the following:

> "At 4 am the Cook jumped overboard having lain in the Moon all night he was out of his head."
> —Logbook, 7/8/1846 *Charles W. Morgan*

> "Sick of darting at whales."
> —Logbook, 7/24/1842, *Charles W. Morgan*

> "at 2 a.m. Joseph B. Thurston apeered on deck a new man to our crew and tacken in the cabin and is acting as 5th mate."
> —Logbook, 5/12/1911, *Charles W. Morgan*

> "Mr. Howland overboard Oars were thrown then and waste boat cleared away ... he went down before we could get to him."
> —Logbook, 12/1/1881, *Charles W. Morgan*

Choosing First and Last Poems

For the first poem in your collection, choose a poem you like, for it will be one of the most read poems in the book. That automatically makes it more important than many others. Also, since the first poem is frequently used as a sample read in impulse purchasing decisions, it may be a good idea if this first poem is not very long.

Normally the first poem starts a conversation with the reader and is often broad, suggestive of the themes and topics raised throughout the book. Maybe it serves as a summary of the pages to follow. Maybe the first poem makes a statement that is being proved (or contradicted) in the successive 50 pages. Maybe it divulges the end result of a journey to be developed in the poems included in the book.

Ideally, the last poem would interact with the first one, for they are the bookends of the collection. If a poetry book were a house and the first poem were the front door, the last poem would be the back door. Thus, the last poem could not only function as something closing the book but also as gateway to different interpretations, making it bigger by raising further questions.

A sense of ending is more important than a sense of closure. As in life, the ending does not have to tie a neat ribbon around the whole thing. The journey does not have to finish with fanfare, victory and forced optimism. A reader can see through that. No less importantly, you'd know that you tried to "redeem" your collection in a disingenuous way.

Poetry Book Boot Camp participant Wendy Jett shares the following:

> My first poem had to be the one I chose, as it was definitely the lead-in to the relationship that the manuscript was about. The last poem was a bit more challenging. I changed it several times and even totally dumped the one that I thought I wanted to finish with because it didn't really give me a sense of resolution that I wanted for the manuscript. I also read my manuscript backwards, end to start, to see how it made me feel and what the flow felt like. It was an interesting thing to do. I was able to see things a bit differently in that order.

Poetry Book Boot Camp participant Bill Verble shares the following:

I selected the first poem since it was short—only six lines—and I thought it would grab the reader's attention. I believe it represents the theme well. The last poem was initially part of a bonded pair that I saw as being a good conclusion to the manuscript. As the manuscript evolved I realized the poem did not fully fit the overall tone of the manuscript, but the other poem in the bonded pair did fit, so I dropped the initial last poem and made the other one in the pair the last poem.

Epilogues

I like epilogues because they give the author an opportunity for multiple endings of the book. Think about the depth and surprise you could add to the end of a poetry collection if you had multiple endings. This could be done in a subtle way. For example, you could arrange the final few poems so that each serves as a last poem, each closing an aspect or a theme. Conversely, every "last" poem could be posing new questions and sparking further conversations beyond the pages of the collection.

You don't have to add a separate section or call it an epilogue, although some poets do just that. Frank X Walker added a section called "Afterword" in his book *Last Will, Last Testament* and in this last section he placed the final poem.

The last poem of Tom C. Hunley's chapbook *Scotch Tape World* is a two-part poem titled "P.S. and P.P.S."

And, OK, fine. In my book *How God Punishes*, I did add a separate section and actually labeled it "Epilogue."

Notes Page

Often poets ask me if they should footnote their poems, or use simpler words, or explain more in the body of the poem. I tend to think that we should not target our poetry to be understood by the largest number of readers. Newspapers have this goal. Poetry is a language art, embracing beauty and efficiency of language. This is not to say that being understood is not an art! I'm saying that I would not compromise language, not in poetry.

Also, I tend to discourage poets from overexplaining in the body of the poem. We want the poem to be elegant in its flow and overexplaining achieves exactly the opposite.

Furthermore, in poetry collections there are better ways to give credit or elaborate on a point than using footnotes. Not all readers will need explanation, and those who do will need the explanation only once. If a footnote is added to the page, it will be there forever. Therefore, I recommend placing any explanations in an endnotes section at the end of the book.

What kind of information belongs on notes pages? Here are a few examples:

- research sources
- foreign words
- borrowed expressions
- specific definitions
- allusions or references to other texts
- inspirations and/or imitations
- stories of how the poems came about

My general recommendation: if in doubt, add information in the notes pages of the manuscript, then discuss with your editor.

To illustrate, below you'll find several excerpts from notes pages of Accents books.

From *Places of Permanent Shade* by J Kates:

"Chart II: Physical Characteristics of the Sea Goddess" (p. 14) and "Chart IV: Abodes of the Sea Goddess" (p. 15) are found poems—the second more intact from its source than the first—drawn from the catalogue of an exhibit in Montréal dedicated to the art and culture of the Inuit people of northern Canada, and focusing on the sea goddess most commonly known by the name of Sedna.

From *The Compost Reader* by Karen Schubert:

"Epistemology of Light" references Gasworks, James Turrell (1993). Mattress Factory, Pittsburgh. Visitors were rolled into an enclosed sphere on their backs.

From *Strictly from Hunger* by Jennifer Litt:

"Tuned Out": The italicized line in stanza two is taken from Joni Mitchell's song "My Old Man" from the album *Blue* (Reprise, 1971).
"Dropping Anchor in Neverland": The italicized lines in stanza two (lines 10–12) were inspired by Peter Pan fanfiction (*An Awfully Big Adventure*, 2003).
"Mother Superior Gets Porked Again": The italicized lines in stanzas three, four, & five define the idiom, strictly from hunger, which became the title of my book.

Poetry Book Boot Camp Participant Manuel Grimaldi shares the following:

Yes, I do have a notes page to cover my tracks on anything I felt where credit was due to a writer, a screenwriter, a playwright (for examples); or to go over, whether they be definitions, brief pop cultural or art history analyses, or titles and phrases that might otherwise appear immediately impenetrable to the casual reader. Confound it, I don't want to confound the confounded language! But as for the notes, I was careful to follow prudence and good judgment throughout for brevity's sake. The notes take up just a page in my collection.

All that said, keep in mind that sometimes a combination of an appropriate title and a strategic epigraph can provide enough background and make an endnote entry unnecessary. When in doubt, ask the opinion of a trusted reader to gauge if you've been able to achieve the desired level of clarity.

Acknowledgments Page

The acknowledgments page gives the author an opportunity to formally express gratitude to the people who have helped in the making of the book. Most often the author thanks the editors of magazines and/or chapbooks where a few of the poems may have previously appeared. You are expected to credit previous publications and a leading sentence of thanks is a graceful way to accomplish this. Most poets list the previously published poems in order of their appearance in the manuscript, although I've seen them arranged in alphabetical or chronological order.

It is customary to express gratitude to the publisher and the cover artist and to acknowledge any grants and organizations that have supported the writing and/or publishing of the book. The author also may mention advance readers, writing group colleagues, mentors, etc.

Do you need an acknowledgments page? It's not mandatory, and if you don't have previously published poems, it might make sense to skip one altogether. It won't hurt you if you don't have publication credits, though a long list of poems that have appeared in various journals signals to the editors that they are reading mature work, meaning that the author has been working on this book for a while.

About the Author Page

This is a dedicated biographical page where a paragraph or more could be added about the author's accomplishments or interests. A part of the function of this information is to show personality, so feel free to include one or more quirky details that inject humor and, at the same time, confidence.

Whenever I read about the author, I love learning where the

poet is from, where she lives, what she does for a living and what her most significant creative accomplishments are.

Some authors include details on how to contact them with feedback or comments. You can put your email address in your bio or, better yet, a link to your website, where interested parties can read relevant, up-to-date and plentiful information about you and your publications.

A few examples of "About the Author" pages are below:

Wendy Jett, the author of *Girl*:

> Wendy Jett is a long time fitness instructor, decoupage nerd, Improv junkie and loves to write. She is a born and raised Kentucky girl and now calls Lexington home. Mom to two humans, Kayla and Stevie and one canine, Lola Jolene, she does the best she can every day! Some days she does better than others.

Yvonne Johnson, the author of *I Am Woman*:

> Yvonne M. Johnson graduated from the University of Kentucky with degrees in English and Computer Science. As an undergraduate, she was inducted as an Affrilachian Poet, served as president of her university's creative writing club, and was managing poetry and German language editor of the undergraduate literary journal. She also holds a master's degree in cyber security from Lancaster University in England, which she completed on a Fulbright scholarship. When she is not writing, she can be found riding horses, training her Labrador to find missing people, and legally hacking into her customers' computer systems.

While most biographical notes are written in the third person, I've come across some excellent first-person narratives that add further immediacy and a personal touch. Here is Jennifer Litt's About the Author page from *Strictly from Hunger*:

> After graduating from the University of Rhode Island with a BA in English, I moved to London, England, to work as an au pair for the

three children of two journalist parents and to absorb the culture. It was a year of surprises: a British ambassador's daughter added to the mix; earning a Diploma of Chelsea College (MA equivalent) in Modern Social and Cultural Studies, and enduring an attack by kittiwakes and guillemots while taking a boat tour with the Royal Bird Watching Society. After returning to the States and earning my secondary teaching certification, I taught high school English in Miami, Florida, and then adult literacy in Rochester, New York, where obtaining Education-through-the-Arts grants and facilitating collaborative literary/literacy projects with other community organizations became my focus.

My mother died less than a month after I turned 50. That year I ran my one and only marathon on Mount Desert Island, Maine, cheered on my son when he rowed for Cornell at Henley-on-Thames, worked as an adjunct writing instructor at several area colleges, and established a writing services business. Cobbling together a living was both freeing and frightening, but it did give me time to write—with poetry gradually edging out fiction. To be closer to my family, I relocated to Fort Lauderdale. Writing and revising *Strictly from Hunger* has taken me several years, but I've enjoyed all aspects of this undertaking. I look forward to new adventures.

Thinking Like a Book Buyer

Have you found yourself at a library, facing the poetry section, choosing a book or two to take home? What has your decision process been? Did you open a book at random and read a few lines? Did you read an entire poem? Was it the first or the last? Consider your own attitudes toward others' collections. What is it that pulls you into a poetry book? Language? Story? Cover image?

I make a distinction between wanting to read a book and wanting to own a book. For example, I aim to own all books published by my students. I've already read most of them before publication, but it gives me enormous joy to keep personal copies. I want to read more books than to own, so sometimes I first read a book before deciding whether to add it to my collection. If I'm interested in reading it again, referring to it, teaching from it, learning from it, I keep it. There is no space for all the books I'd like to own, so I need to be judicious. Fiction writers have solved the problem with electronic books, but poetry is lagging behind and insists on physical books as concrete objects, perhaps in an attempt to counteract the abstract aspects of poetry.

A solid influence on my purchasing decision is a recommendation from a person whose opinion I respect, though I've made many an impulse decision browsing the poetry shelves at bookstores. I normally read the title, open the book at random and sample a poem or two. No narrative arc plays a role here, just my personal taste and level of intrigue. Emotional engagement with the work is normally enough for me to buy it, but if I add the suspicion that I might be able to learn something and improve my own writing by reading this book, that makes the particular collection irresistible.

There will be those who read from beginning to end and those who read from the end to the beginning, but not at the bookstore. (Well ... let me contradict myself with an outlier. In 2014 my book *How God Punishes* came out in Bulgarian. My father walked into a bookstore, picked up my book, read it there from beginning to end, then put it back and left without actually buying it. *Katerina will give one to me for free*, he reasoned, and I did.) Readers normally would only sample poems from the book there at the bookstore. Even a formal poetry reading or a book launch is a sampling.

We have no control over the random sample that the potential reader selects in order to make a purchasing decision. However, we can deliberately prepare *a* sample for the readers-to-be.

What should this sample contain? I believe that you can learn a lot by reading the title, the table of contents, and the first and the last poem. Try it with an unfamiliar book and see if you agree.

What does this sample say about your manuscript? Is it in line with your intention for the work?

If desired, share your sample with a poet from your writers' group and ask them what they've been able to surmise about the collection, based solely on the sample. How do you feel about their findings?

In my Poetry Book Boot Camp workshops, I match participants two by two and give them the assignment of exchanging manuscript samples. The participants then have a conversation where they share with each other the reactions and questions based only on the manuscript sample consisting of title, table of contents, and first and last poems.

Poetry Book Boot Camp participant Quincy Gray McMichael shares the following about her experience of swapping manuscript samples with another poet:

> I was surprised to experience the grounding effect of preparing my first poem, last poem, and table of contents (TOC). This exercise balanced my own understanding of my manuscript in what it really is about, where it needs to begin, and where the narrative lands.
>
> In turn, the practice of exchanging drafts and examining my partner's manuscript illuminated for me the ways in which I could better situate my own TOC and poems. My partner's feedback helped me to see my writing and arrangement in a new light.
>
> I now recommend that any poet who has an early-stage collection on their desk print the first poem, last poem, and TOC—then sit down with a nice mug of tea and a fresh pair of eyes and see what reveals itself. If you have a writing partner to exchange drafts with, even better.

For the manuscript sample exercise, Quincy was partnered with poet Mary Elizabeth Moore, who had this to share about the experience:

We were to exchange samples—title, table of contents, and first and last poems. Thus, I could not send my partner a pile of poems; I would have to focus, make decisions, focus again. The assignment posed the very questions I had been asking myself: which poems to include, how to order them, and what to share in the beginning and end. With a basket of questions, my partner and I took the giant step toward composing our respective books.

My partner's manuscript was profound. I admired the chronological-thematic flow of her poems as she explored experiences of struggle and resilience. I grew as a poet as I closely read her work. She, in turn, read my work with a sharp eye, discerning the passions at its core. She highlighted strengths that I did not recognize, and she offered significant questions and suggestions, to which I still return.

Manuscript Worksheet

If keeping organized gives you a sense of safety, then the following exercise might feel grounding to you. You can add the information to your meta file or just do the exercise on a piece of paper to see which questions present you with more difficulties.

The working title of my manuscript is _____
   because _____.

It is a collection of ____ poems written over the past ____
   months/years.

The main themes of the book are _____
   _____.

The collection starts with the poem _____
   because _____.

The collection ends with the poem _____ because
   _____.

   _____

(IF) The collection is divided into the following sections:

_____ explores _____

_____.

_____ explores _____

_____.

_____ explores _____

_____.

_____ explores _____

_____.

The audience of this book is _____

_____.

Poet Glenna Meeks was kind enough to share the worksheet that she filled out while working on her manuscript during the Poetry Book Boot Camp workshop:

The working title of my manuscript is **The Black Madonna** because **I'm black and all my mother figures were**.

It is a collection of **Mothering poems** written over the past **10 years**.

The main themes of the book are **being mothered and mothering as a black woman in America**.

The collection starts with the poem "**A Street I Call Serenity**" **because it was a time in my life when my life was simple and uncomplicated**. The collection ends with the poem "**I Write**" because **it wraps up my life and explains how I make sense of it all**.

(IF) The collection is divided into the following sections:

My grandmother who was my primary caregiver and explores **who she was and my care of her at the end of life**.

_____

My mother and who she was and explores **who she was to me.**

My two great-grandmothers and my aunt and who they were and explores **who they were to me.**

The last section is about me and my challenge of becoming a mother and explores **how I mothered my children.**

The audience of this book is **women who are mothers or want to be mothers**.

Glenna had the following words to add:

> This book craft class taught me how to organize my poems into a manuscript that was organized by the principle of writing in series. When I looked over all the poems I had written over the years there was a clear subject that most of the poems were about and it was mothering. In addition, I was taught how to organize by sections, the foreword, the table of contents and acknowledgment pages. I was taught to consider the best first poem, the best last poem, best title and where to put the best title poem. The differences in types of poetry books based on the number of pages and the advantage and disadvantage of each. I was taught what to consider when choosing a publisher and entering a contest.

Qualities Needed at This Stage

Flexibility in what you consider progress. If you spend two months arranging your manuscript in a particular order, then you decide that you don't like the result and go back to square one, is this progress? It absolutely is. It's also information. And, if you receive information that you haven't made progress, this is also progress. In this kind of work, a step in any direction is a step forward and also an act of courage, especially if you don't even know where "forward" might be.

Willingness to try out various approaches. With regular

snapshots, there is virtually zero risk in trying out new arrangements and testing outrageous architectures. Even if you think that you've erected a solid castle, topple it and build a new one. The potential payoff is tremendous. The downside is time "wasted." But if you were not willing to waste time, you wouldn't have come this far, right?

PART 3

Revision

What's Next?

Assuming you've caught up on all assignments, by now you should have a draft of a poetry collection with a working title, arranged in some order that is *good enough for now*. In the process you may have aggregated a file with poems you have set aside that could potentially be added later.

If you have followed the advice to refrain from editing, and if you've been itching to do so, now is the time.

During this stretch of the process, our goal is to polish the manuscript and to craft it into a version that is *good enough to start submitting*. Note that *good enough to start submitting* does not mean finished. If your manuscript is accepted, in many cases that does not mean finished either. Upon acceptance, your editor may request changes. Or the production schedule may be so long that you continue writing and revising and at some point you feel the need to request changes. What I'm saying is—in my experience—published means finished, having it in fixed form.

Now is the time to write the rest of the "missing poems," those gaps you identified in the previous section. Even if you feel you've already followed up, a few late arrivals might surprise you. You may find yourself not only adding but also replacing poems—swapping older ones for newer ones.

You may be streamlining your collection; you may be balancing the themes. You may be digging through details, hunting for inconsistencies, pondering over punctuation decisions. You may be verifying you grammar. Just kidding! Checking if you're paying attention. You may be fine-tuning your table of contents. You may be making a lasting decision—albeit not necessarily final—about your manuscript title.

Those of you with "mature work" have an advantage. If you belong to a writers' group or you've frequented poetry classes and workshops where you've had opportunities to receive feedback on individual poems, this stretch of the schedule could be significantly shorter for you.

The Value of Workshop

I cannot believe it took me so long to mention the big three again. I might be preaching to the choir, but if I did not underscore the importance of the big three, I would feel incomplete. These, of course, are reading, writing, and receiving feedback.

Forgive Me for a Few Personal Paragraphs

I started attending writing groups in elementary school. I remember walking into the room and everyone seemed giant. They were high school students. I felt out of my league and mostly confused by the conversation, so after a few meetings I gave up. It was too soon for me. Several years later I returned. I was in high school myself and had published a poem in a national literary journal. At that point I started attending weekly writing groups and workshopping poems. I regularly received reading recommendations, studied other poets' work, and shared my own work. The weekly meetings kept me on a schedule. I would try to bring something every week, and even if I didn't, I still went, for these poets became my friends. I had found people like me, even though we were all different ages: from me—the youngest—to retirees and every age in between. Different walks of life too: from me—a high schooler—to college students, soldiers, a colonel, a pilot, a nurse, a sailor, a couple of teachers, a librarian. That pilot decades later became the president of Bulgaria. This is no joke! See what writers' groups can do for you? That sailor became my first ex-husband. See what writers' groups can do to you? Not only did I attend poetry discussions but I also regularly participated in group activities—organized readings, trips to various cities for events and meetings with other creative people. I became a part of a community—my first literary community of sharing and caring.

As I am writing this, I'm overcome with gratitude and happiness at having received this gift of poetry and genuine friendship. That experience left a mark on my development not only as a poet but also as a human being. I cannot imagine life without participating in and contributing to a literary community.

Fast forward to 2007, when I, with the help of songwriter Colin Watkins, started a group in Lexington—Poezia. That means "poetry" in Bulgarian. "Free and open to everyone who loves the art of writing." We met every Thursday at 7 p.m. in Common Grounds Coffee Shop. Whoever wanted to participate could show up—typically around 10 people. I met hundreds of poets that way, made wonderful friends. The group meant so much to so many people. We had our principles written up on a card, kind of like a membership card. Poet Jay McCoy prepared it and gave each of us a copy. Please see the photos of the somewhat worn-out card that I still carry in my wallet (photos of front and back shown below).

I included this information because I believe we need each other. Poetry is often written in solitude and shared in community, and in order to have a true creative balance, a poet needs a

Poezia...

...is free & open to everyone who loves writing

...welcomes people from all writing levels and all walks of life; everyone is equal here – equally respected, nurtured and loved

- we are present
- we want to be here
- we bring positive energy to the group
- we listen respectfully
- we wait for the other person to finish talking before we speak
- we are here to improve ourselves
- there is always only one conversation at a time
- we hear critique with gratitude and respect regardless if we agree with it or not

community, even if it consists of just two other members of a writers' group.

Tacit and Explicit Knowledge

Poetry has always been my one true love, though at some point I considered committing to the field of artificial intelligence. Specifically, having a machine understand a human question and seamlessly produce a meaningful answer, parsing and understanding language, optimizing communication, etc., seemed fascinating to me. During those years I researched and programmed a few "expert systems"—interactive programs that through a series of questions were able to present the user with relevant data or advice. In every one of these cases, the critical success factor was to be able to convert tacit knowledge into explicit instruction.

The kind of knowledge that one can clearly articulate in oral or written form is called explicit knowledge. For example, a textbook contains explicit knowledge. Tacit knowledge is the type that doesn't readily yield to clear and easy definition. Tacit means silent. For example, intuition is a type of tacit knowledge.

I believe that the path to mastery of writing poetry is the journey from tacit to explicit to tacit again. If we do not want to call it mastery, fine—let's call it a degree of proficiency.

Part of the creative writing teacher's job is to make the tacit knowledge explicit in the form of repeatable, talk-about-able steps. This is exactly what we're doing in this book. We're unpacking the amorphous, loaded, intimidating process of "putting a poetry book together" and making as much of it as possible less abstract.

To describe my personal poetic journey in one sentence: I wrote and edited on instinct, then during my time at the Naslund-Mann Graduate School of Writing, I learned a host of specific editing skills, which I later internalized. On my first day of my first workshop in my MFA program, I could hardly follow the conversation. Even though I had spent more than a decade in the United States, I was not proficient with literary terminology, so a critical part of the class discussion was locked in a foreign language. Worse, the participants were quoting authors and books I'd never heard of, and all I could do was to try to scribble things down and hide my feelings of inadequacy. Our workshop leader, poet Greg Pape, was both experienced and compassionate, and he taught us about a very specific and manageable tool that helped me come up to speed—the revision checklist. I use it to this day and recommend it to anyone who is asking the eternal question "How do I know if a poem is finished?"

Revision Checklist

A revision checklist is a series of activities and tests that a poet performs as part of the editing process. Revision checklists eventually get internalized, and poets automatically perform the checks. I want to share with you several checklist items I'd recommend before a poem is put aside as "finished."

TITLE. Does the title work, and by "work," I mean does the title perform a function? A simple test is to read the poem without the title and see if you are missing anything. If it makes no difference whether you read the poem with or without the title, then the title does no heavy lifting. To me, a good title gives extra information which is relevant to the poem, yet it is not repeated in the poem's body.

PERSPECTIVE. Who is speaking? The choice of perspective creates or removes distance between the poet and the speaker and thus makes certain poems easier (or even possible) to write. What are your choices, besides first person? To me, writing poems is a form of speaking to myself, so I quite frequently use a second person perspective.

FORM. Form is the container for your content and lineation can make or break your poems. I believe that content comes first, then lineation shapes it into a form. Before you call a poem finished, you could consider if there might be another form that could work just as well or even better. At the very least, if you've written a poem in short lines, you can try it with long lines and vice versa. In different forms, different elements become visible, and some wonderful editing could happen. And unlike juggling porcelain cups, experimenting with form in poetry is virtually risk-free. If you don't like the result, you can always revert to the previous version. In my classes I ask the participants to submit poems in two different forms, and part of the discussion is devoted to comparing the advantages and the disadvantages of each. I want to make clear that in this context I'm using the term "form" broadly. Pouring content from one free-form container to another is just as fascinating as shifting a pantoum into a villanelle. Ultimately, my belief is that the form should highlight and support the content.

LINEATION. There is a lot that can be said for the art of lineation and its considerations and nuances. I'd recommend that—if you haven't already—you devote some time to read specialized books to really understand the purpose and workings of the poetic line. Lineation shows a level of skill and attention to detail like nothing else. Here I will list just three points to keep in mind:

- Line length goes a long way in supporting or disrupting the tone of the poem.
- Creating tension at the end of a line and resolving that

tension on a subsequent line can keep the poem surprising and fresh to hold the reader's interest.

- It is within your power to make your poems look beautiful. Just as you take a few seconds to enjoy the appealing appearance of your food on your plate at mealtime, in a similar way a reader reacts to a poem on the page before they read it. Remember that the size of a computer document page varies from the size of the printed page, and sometimes carefully considered shape poems do not transfer well in print or need to be reimagined.

SYNTAX AND REAL ESTATE. The way you construct your sentences has the ability to highlight certain words and expressions. For example, you could say:

Today I went to the post office.
I went to the post office today.
To the post office today I went.

Location, location, location. Are the most important words and phrases at the most important places?

WHAT IS VISUALLY IMPORTANT? Open a book of poems and thumb through it without actually reading the poems just to determine where your glance naturally settles and which words you read first. Whatever looks different—or otherwise stands out—holds elevated visual significance. Extra-long lines, phrases formatted in different styles, end-lines of stanzas, and extra spacing are some examples. As part of following an editing checklist, make sure you highlight the lines, words and phrases you meant to draw attention to.

REPETITION. I experienced my first decade of workshops and writing groups in Bulgaria, which has a somewhat different school of poetry. I remember one of my early mentors, Yanaki Petrov, teaching me two rules about poetry that I internalized and I still tend to apply. I no longer subscribe to these rules 100 percent, but they greatly influenced the way I examine and edit poems.

1. A poem should be composed of the fewest words possible.

This is a statement of economy of language and language precision. A poem doesn't necessarily need to be short, but the better friends we are with language, the more elegant our expression becomes, increasing the likelihood of dressing our intentions in fewer words. Enough said?

2. You should not have any words repeated within a poem.

Repetition is a powerful tool for creating rhythm and patterns. That said, let's make sure every repetition is intentional. Often, beginner poets need to be alerted to unintentional, unconscious repetitions within their work. At that point they have a choice—to diversify language or to deliberately keep the repetition, even enhance it.

Part of the checklist, then, is scrubbing for "lazy" writing and taking this opportunity to upgrade language wherever needed.

TENSE. Many poems are written in present tense. Still, it might be a good idea to consciously decide if that is, in fact, the best choice. Present tense affords more immediacy, but in certain cases (such as a poem with flashbacks or forward leaps), it might make sense to keep it respectively in the past or in the future. A common issue is for an author to start a poem in one tense and at some point to inadvertently shift into another tense. A simple check should solve the problem.

GRAMMAR AND PUNCTUATION. I don't think there is a "one-size-fits-all" solution here. If you forego punctuation, however, keep in mind that your line breaks will have to step up to perform double duty. Impeccable grammar and punctuation do lead the reader along and create better clarity, but that is not always the goal in mind. The poet may want to keep the reader guessing with all the possibilities.

SOUND/RHYTHM/RHYME. To many readers, poetry is especially satisfying whenever they encounter musicality in the language, various overt and inner rhymes, assonances and alliterations. Some of these harmonious delights arrive on first draft by instinct. Others are intentionally sought and edited into the lines. Different languages operate differently due to word length specifics and vowel-consonant ratios. English, with its numerous words, has such an incredible wealth of synonyms that in almost all cases a poet has several options to fine-tune the sound of the poem to match its reason.

GIVING CREDIT. Is there a line, an expression, a source of inspiration or any other reason you need to acknowledge another person, event, or work of art? If in doubt, give credit. Nobody has won by being ungenerous. Credit can be given in a footnote, on notes pages or in an epigraph or simply by mentioning the name of the person or the work as a part of the text of the poem. In the previous section you can find real-life examples of notes pages entries.

CLARITY. Yes, in poetry you can lean on the reader to connect the dots, to dance with withheld information. Still, if the reader is at a complete loss, she might stop reading, because at the very least she'd feel that she's not the audience for this work. In classes I ask the participants to let the poet know at what place they'd have stopped reading if they didn't have to read the poem for workshop. A good reader would point out to you any unclarities or areas of confusion, and then it would be up to you.

ENDING. How does the ending close the poem? Think about the last open mic you attended. For certain poems, you may have needed visual cues to understand when the poem is over. For example, the poet said "thank you" or stepped away from the mic or shuffled papers. There were other poems where you did not need help to understand that the poem had ended. The ending nailed it shut. This is what I mean here. Where is the real finale of the poem you are editing?

TITLE, FIRST LINE, LAST LINE CHECK. There is a test I perform, and on some poems it works beautifully. Reading the poem title, first line and last line often can give sort of a summary of the poem. I don't know what other value this information has besides that it's satisfying whenever it works, and it may help point toward the real ending of the poem.

HAVE YOU WRITTEN THE ENTIRE POEM? For years on my radio show, *Accents*, I asked all my guests who taught creative writing, "What is the most important thing you teach your students?" and Kentucky poet and writer George Ella Lyon's answer was "Let it emerge." Sometimes we need more time or more courage or even more poetic skill in order to put certain events or attitudes on paper. The questions to ask here are "Have I written the entire poem?" and "Is there anything else I want to say?" Note that if the answer to the latter question is "yes," that does not necessarily mean you need to be adding to the poem you're currently editing. It might mean that a new poem is on its way, perhaps as part of a bonded pair.

BEGINNER-WRITER GIVEAWAYS. This may irk a number of people, but I would feel incomplete if I did not include a list of beginner-writer giveaways. These are expressions and mannerisms a more experienced writer typically grows out of. This list is by no means exhaustive, and I do not aim to embarrass anyone; I'm also guilty of publishing a few poems that include items from the list. Part of this giveaway collection simply reveals my personal editorial and aesthetic prejudice, so staying connected to the reason for the poem is your best guide. Now that I've written an entire paragraph apologizing for my opinion, here it is.

- The word "thousand" as a substitute for "many."
- Ending a poem with the word "tongue."
- Ellipsis anywhere in the poem.
- Cliches such as "tall grass," "pale moon," "beneath the skin."
- The word "forever."
- Centering a poem for no reason.
- Using a copyright sign when submitting work for publication.
- Using "creative" fonts and font sizes.
- Work that just generally looks unedited.

OVEREDITING. Overediting is like overwatering plants. It will kill them. Again, it's important to keep in mind the reason for the poem. At all times stay connected to the sometimes vague feeling, the impetus that prompted you to write the poem in the first place. I believe that whenever you edit without being mindful of the reason for the poem, there is a danger of overediting. You could edit the poem to the point of no return. It would look like a poem and act like a poem, but it would hold no energy for you. Your writing group would praise it, maybe it would even get published, but you would feel indifferent. The poem's spark will have been edited out. I call these zombie poems.

What to Do with All These Revisions?

There are many reasons to stay organized. When you start gathering work for a particular project, you want to know exactly where to go to access the latest revisions of your poems, instead of encountering multiple versions in multiple places. You shouldn't need to read and compare and make micro decisions during the stage of macro decisions. This could slow you down, distract you and frustrate you. Ask me how I know.

Worse, a week after book publication, you could come across a forgotten folder containing poems that would have fit beautifully into the manuscript. That would be truly tragic because these poems will likely be "orphans" at this point. If you'd published a themed book and these poems had been part of the theme, they resemble travelers who missed the best train to their destination. Don't ask me how I know.

So, how to keep organized.

I haven't seen a truly foolproof method, but here is what I do with my poems, and it has worked reasonably well over the years.

I draft on paper. I still love a good pen and intentionally selected notebook that visually complements my writing life at the time. I love the ritual of going into a store and falling in love with a notebook that seems hospitable to my words.

Poets have differing attitudes toward their notepads, notebooks and journals. Some plan to keep them forever and leave them behind as a legacy to their descendants; others save them "for now" and end up holding on to them for decades. My practice is different, perhaps influenced by several years of frequent moving that I experienced in my forties. I write quite a bit in journals and notepads and periodically—several times a year—go through everything and perform a procedure I call "harvesting the journals." I read through, looking for anything I might want to keep—usable lines, drafts of poems, ideas I've written down—and transfer anything valuable to the computer. The papers I shred, burn, or recycle. The thought of dying or becoming incapacitated in some way and not having creative control over my own work is terrifying to me.

Once I interviewed Kentucky poet Steve Cope about his book *Selected Poems*, published by Broadstone Books. I asked him, "Isn't it a little early—aren't you too young?" and he said, "Perhaps, but I wanted to be the one to make the selections." I get it!

Ultimately, my journals end up becoming my books. I keep from my journals only what I want to publish and/or what I want to revise at some point in order to publish. Once I adopted this approach, everything became much simpler. I needed to keep a lot less. It was workable, accessible. Suddenly the notes in my journals became manageable.

Whenever I actively work on a book, I make it a point to go through all notebooks and paper material that may have amassed since my last "harvest." In that way, I perform due diligence in making sure I don't miss out on a poem, or even a portion of a poem, or as much as an idea for a poem.

There is a danger associated with keeping the work on paper for too long. Work that is still on paper is virtually unusable for your manuscript. The notebooks could be misplaced, lost or forgotten. Impossible to back up, they are susceptible to being destroyed by fire, flood or mold or to being eaten by rats. Whenever too many notebooks stay "unharvested" for too long, one might dread ploughing through, and this resistance will further slow down the poet.

So, if your work is on paper, first it needs to get lifted into a word processor. Create a file for each poem. The name of this file could be the working title of the poem, and in the file, stack all revisions of the poem FILO (first in, last out) style. In that way, whenever you open the file, you will immediately see the most current revision of the poem. Furthermore, if you scroll down, you can witness the evolution and shapeshifting of the work, and you can backtrack to a previous revision if necessary.

Editing the Manuscript as an Entity

At this stage your focus will shift to microdetails and to the practice of examining, noticing and deciding. You will start zooming in on details and troubleshooting inconsistencies. I believe that consistency (as long as it's not detrimental to the integrity of the individual poems) demonstrates attention to detail and due diligence in editing.

Keep in mind that when working at the book level, all your **local decisions have a global impact**—that is, every choice inside an individual poem needs to be considered against the whole manuscript.

For example, if most poems are from the point of view of a 60-year-old woman and one poem is from the point of view of a six-year-old boy, then make sure this shift is not accidental but a conscious choice. This poem—because it's so different—will stand out from the rest and you should make sure it belongs in the manuscript and serves a purpose. Or you may find out that it needs further revisions.

If all poems are written in third person, and then one or two are in first or second person, see if it might make sense to revise the outliers to have all in third person.

If all poems in the manuscript have foregone punctuation, it would look odd to include just one with punctuation. If you do, I suggest you have a good reason to keep it that way.

Now you can devote time to **fine-tuning how the TOC reads**. You can play with the length of the titles. There is no rule that the entire title needs to be listed on the TOC, so you could select only the beginning (or a portion) of the title to better suit your needs. Conversely, you could go back to the poem and edit the title in order to have a better TOC flow if that's important to you. I do it. To me, it's part of the "manuscript finishing checklist."

Here are several particularly delightful TOC sequences.
From *Biblia Pauperum* by T. Crunk:

III. A Theatre of Fine Devices

Of Salt / Of Dust
Of the Wheel / Of Clay
Of Fire / Of Wind
Of the Blind / Of This World
Of Snow / Of Night
Of the Father / Of Thorns
Of Hands

From *Final Exam* by Andrew Merton:

IV.

Piano Lessons
Feral Pianos
The Anvil and the Steinway Grand
The Lid

From *Etcetera's Mistress* by Thom Ward:

The Howhatwhywherewhen Bone

The Howhatwhywherewhen Bone
The Ballet of the Howhatwhywherewhen Bone
The Contraband of the Howhatwhywherewhen Bone
The Ontological Argument of the Howhatwhywherewhen
    Bone
The Politics of the Howhatwhywherewhen Bone
The Propaganda of the Howhatwhywherewhen Bone
The Birth of the Howhatwhywherewhen Bone
The Invention of How
The Invention of What
The Invention of Why

The Invention of Where
The Invention of When
The Invention of Who

From *I Will Let You Down*, a manuscript by Poetry Book Boot Camp Participant Manuel Grimaldi:

1.
When beaches in Andalucía weep in winters
I turn raindrops into castanets
And I like that
Be with me while I am going
Moonswimming
What Are You Doing New Year's Eve?
In a daydream
Eating a wedding cake

Check the manuscript for **unintentionally repeated words**. Unfortunately, more often than not, it takes the eye of an unbiased reader to point out the unconscious overuse of certain words or expressions in a manuscript. Once you've been alerted, however, you can determine if further editing is necessary.

One efficient method is to highlight every occurrence of the particular word or phrase and evaluate on a case-by-case basis. You will be able to eliminate part of the repetitions immediately and effortlessly. Another part you may have to consider and edit in order to diversify language. The final portion you might decide to leave as they are, making the repetition a conscious choice.

In general, prepare to **read your manuscript many times**. It would be good if a few of these readthroughs happen out loud.

Reading your entire book from beginning to end in one sitting, out loud, is a step I wouldn't skip. If for some reason you're unable to do it yourself, ask someone else to read your book (or a portion of it) to you. It will be helpful, I promise. You will hear different things. For most of my books, I've made audio recordings of my readthroughs prior to publication, even though I've never gone back to listen to the audio. I like the idea of having saved the energy of the voice, the excitement and the pre-publication anxiety.

Poet Kathleen Gregg shares the following:

> Reading my entire manuscript, *Love in Absentia*, in one sitting turned out to be invaluable. I was able to feel whether the poems flowed together well. I was able to notice any gaps in the narrative I was trying to develop. Poems that just didn't belong stood out. I ended up adding new poems and discarding others. I rearranged the order of the poems. These changes definitely improved the manuscript.

Poet Lisa Miller has this to say:

> The advice (which intuitively I took as direction that I'd better not skip, though it seemed logically necessary) to read my entire manuscript out loud, in one sitting, turned out to be very useful. Not only could I suddenly hear tones in my writing—less obvious from the voice in my head alone—I could also see myself reading to a live audience.
>
> And then the vital questions: "Do I really want to be the voice and face of this poem—this narrative—this way?"
>
> Sometimes the answer *yes* inspired me toward more depth on a theme—even a new bonded poem in the collection; otherwise it felt wise to edit, toss, and fine-tune.
>
> Reading a poem aloud is a must; reading the manuscript aloud without breaking the flow is essential to accurately hear, see, and properly digest it.

Streamlining

In most cases, **fine-tuning the order** continues beyond the first few manuscript revisions.

I usually read from the top, beginning to end, and mark each poem that seems out of place or that I feel might work better at a different location in the manuscript. I like to put a sticky note on these pages, so when I gather back my stack of papers, I can immediately see how many poems need relocating and if they seem "clustered" in a particular section. Whenever I swap poems, or find better positions for them, I often physically feel a sense of relief, which is a somatic indication that I've removed a block in the manuscript and supported the flow. Some of you will immediately relate and will completely understand; others will find it weird. Note that I'm not saying it's not weird.

Whenever writing in series, poets may end up with more than enough work that addresses the same issue. I consider it part of the streamlining process to decide the fate of the **overly similar poems**. For example, in my first book, *The Air Around the Butterfly*, I had three poems describing my mother's funeral. I decided that three was too many and only used two of them, the ones that I thought best served my book. Sadly, the poem that I removed never got used in a collection or got published elsewhere and likely never will. That said, I still feel that pulling it out of the manuscript was the right decision.

Feedback

At this point I recommend sharing the collection with a trusted reader. You can always find a mentor to read it and provide feedback. There are plenty of poets who do this for a living, and if you can afford it, you will likely hear helpful ideas and opinions.

Here I'm talking about swapping your collection with a peer who has a book in a similar stage as yours. This is one of the advantages of belonging to writing groups or having long-term literary friendships.

Providing feedback for a manuscript differs from providing feedback on individual poems. In a manuscript swap, you are not expected to provide detailed notes on individual poems, unless, of course, you want to.

Here are the guidelines I recommend when reviewing someone else's work:

> Print the manuscript, read it, take notes on the pages as your thoughts, reactions, and ideas for improvements occur. Don't wait to reach the end before taking notes. Your unedited reaction is valuable. At the end of your read-through, write down your comments on what worked well as a whole and what is still in need of editing.
>
> Do you have any thoughts about the organization of the manuscript?
>
> Any poems out of place? Ideas about reordering?
>
> Were you able to identify anything missing in terms of content?
>
> What is your reaction to the combination of title, first poem and last poem?
>
> What did the table of contents tell you about the book you were about to read?
>
> Did you identify any weak poems in the manuscript? Is there anything that does not measure up to the quality of this body of work? Do not be afraid to provide this feedback. It's probably the biggest gift you could give your fellow poet.

You can have an in-person meeting or a phone call or you could provide written feedback. My personal preference is for real-time feedback because that allows follow-up questions, changes of opinion, or discussions of ideas as they come up.

Warning One: Becoming Discouraged by Feedback

The sad truth is that often we don't need a lot of discouragement in order to give up on our projects. Sometimes not feeling encouraged or understood is enough, especially if we've shared work at a vulnerable stage. On these pages, I've kept repeating that most importantly, you need to remain connected to the reason for the writing, to the reason you wrote this piece in the first place. Although it's wonderful to receive praise and support along the way, you need to remember that others are not responsible for your writing. Your writing is your own responsibility at every stage, including protecting it from untimely or inadequate critique. Do I need to repeat that you should not take feedback personally? Very well, then: you should not take feedback personally.

Warning Two: Perfectionism Paradise

In the editing stage, where your task is to polish individual poems, as well as the manuscript as a whole, you could get trapped in perfectionism. This is unfortunate, because you cannot please perfectionism, and overly high standards sometimes can be used as an excuse to not finish a project. Additionally, at this stage you could also get derailed by seeking too much feedback. Seeking too much feedback might signal insecurity and needing someone else's stamp of approval. Additionally, various readers could offer vastly different feedback and send the author thrashing in opposing directions.

Signs That the Manuscript Is Not Ready

1. You know it. If you have worked on your poetry long enough, chances are you have developed a degree of internal

honesty about your work. Wanting your manuscript to be finished doesn't make it so. If there is a sad, quiet voice in you that sighs, "I know it's not ready" do not submit it for publication. Instead, send it out to a trusted reader for comments and constructive feedback.

2. You don't like it. Do not send out a manuscript you don't like. There is no way you can win in this scenario. If it gets rejected, you will feel stupid for sending it out in the first place. If it gets accepted, you open a whole new can of worms. Instead of submitting it, put it aside for a while. Take a break from the manuscript but continue working on your writing. Then, after some time has passed, you may be able to make a better decision about the work—whether to edit, recycle in a different genre or simply let go.

3. You change it drastically and often. If every time you put your hands on your manuscript it gets reconceptualized, reordered, renamed, reenvisioned or otherwise majorly revised, I am so sorry, but it's not ready. Do not send it. If an older, "inferior" version of it gets accepted, you will regret your own impatience. Instead, wait for the manuscript to settle.

4. You keep on writing more and more poems on the main topic. Do yourself a favor and spend the energy writing rather than collecting. Don't close the manuscript. Maybe you will be able to write a full-length book rather than a chapbook. Maybe you will be able to replace older, weaker poems with newer and better ones. Maybe you will come up with new ideas for structure. In any case, if you are writing, keep on writing. You will have time to consider the collection later.

5. The manuscript has all your poems. If the manuscript you are about to submit for publication contains all the poems you've ever written, I can almost guarantee it's not ready. As part of a poet's growth, you will have had the need and the

opportunity to let go of work that you've outgrown either as a creator or as a person. If you haven't been through such a process yet, your manuscript is not ready, no matter how ready you feel to start submitting.

Signs That the Manuscript Is Ready

1. You like it. To me, the number one sign of readiness is that you yourself like your own manuscript. You are its most important reader and audience, first and foremost.

2. There is a lightbulb of joy in your heart at the thought of sharing your work. That said, there might be another lightbulb flashing with horror and anxiety. That is perfectly normal and might indicate that you're closer than ever to being public with your work. For such occasions, I've come up with a little rhyming expression in Bulgarian: „Ако се страхувам, значи си струва." "If I'm afraid, that means it's worth it."

3. You know that this is, indeed, your best effort and will continue to be so for some time. You might be starting a new job or switching writing efforts to the novel you've been dreaming about. You may be in a now-or-never or now-or-not-in-the-following-few-years type of situation. If that's the case, it's worth submitting and attempting to publish the work.

4. You've reached the point of diminishing returns. The law of diminishing returns is a term in economics and largely states that once a certain level of quality is reached, additional improvements do not majorly enhance the work—in other words, putting in more effort would not yield much of a result. It is also known as piddling, overediting, and getting lost in the details.

All this reading, editing, steeping in minutia sounds like a lot of work, and it is. Still, let's not forget one of the critical keywords describing a project: "temporary." At some point there should be an end. The most common, most effective reason to wrap up your collection into a sendable state comes in the form of a submission deadline, and you want to give your manuscript a chance to be considered. Furthermore, while the work is under consideration, you can really take a break because, in effect, you have transferred the question "Is my manuscript ready?" to somebody else's inbox.

Qualities Needed at This Stage

Ability for sustained and focused attention. Here the poet needs to be a jeweler—not a jeweler of a single diamond but of an entire necklace or a tiara. Here the poet needs to reconcile details of the individual poems with the details and the concept of the whole.

Willingness to seek, hear and consider feedback. I'm not suggesting that you need to agree with every opinion you receive. That would be counterproductive. Bulgarian people have an expression about such situations: "Many grandmas—skinny baby." I'm suggesting that hearing the feedback and weighing it against the reason for the work goes a long way.

PART 4

Publication

Where to Meet Publishers in Person

The time has come to start talking about publishing. This could be the most daunting part, because so much is out of your control and up to other people. There are abundant opportunities to learn the hard way, so try not to go through this process in isolation, but find a mentor or talk to a poet friend who has published books already.

Where do publishers hang out, and how can you meet them and get to be on a first-name basis?

Publishers, like other professionals, attend **conferences**—regional and national alike. They often participate in publishing panels or sit behind tables at book fairs. At events such as the Association of Writers & Writing Programs Conference (AWP), for example, you can personally meet and talk to actual decision-makers by browsing the book fair and stopping by the exhibitors' booths. You can introduce yourself, ask questions, exchange cards and follow up with emails after the conference.

Various poetry events are another excellent venue. Publishers love poetry and do attend readings. A friend of mine, Marianne Peel, tells the story of how once she read several poems at an open mic event at the Kentucky State Poetry Society conference, and after the reading, Virginia Underwood, the publisher of Shadelandhouse Modern Press, handed Marianne a business card on which she had written, "I want to work with you." I have a similar story myself, where a reading from my first book led to the publishing of my second, *The Porcupine of Mind*, by Broadstone Books and my lasting friendship with publisher Larry Moore.

Therefore, my recommendation is to not miss an opportunity to read in public. You never know who might be listening.

How to find out about poetry and other literary events? Signing up for the newsletters of leading local literary organizations would be a great way to start. Also following several especially active authors on social media would give you more than enough to get started in attending events and getting to know people in person. My mentor Molly Peacock tells the story of her first steps in her literary community. She would give herself the assignment of talking to one person after each literary event. Everyone needs to start somewhere, and seemingly small steps do add up.

Where to Submit Your Manuscript

In this book, I will primarily discuss how to submit your manuscript with the goal of publishing a poetry book rather than covering in depth how to send out individual poems for consideration by magazines and journals, although I will touch upon the latter.

If you belong to a writers' group, ask your friends where they've been sending their work. If your poet friends have already published books or are currently in the process of publication, you can start by submitting to the same places. Often poets with a similar aesthetic and at a similar career level gravitate toward one another, so if a publisher likes your peers' work, there is a good chance they might enjoy your writing as well.

Make sure to ask your friends if they actually recommend the press. Inquire what it was like to work with a particular publisher and if they'd submit a manuscript to them again, knowing what they know now. I am in the habit of posing two questions: "What was your experience?" and "Do you recommend them as a publisher?" Then, based on the person's response, or the lack thereof, you can make an informed decision.

Once you've identified an appropriate publisher, it may help if you have a contact at the press—someone who could place your manuscript on the right desk, so to say. True, many small poetry presses comprise one, two or three people working from their homes, so in that case this manuscript placing may look more like email forwarding. Still, having your manuscript read by a decision-maker is a win, especially if you are able to have it considered despite the press's blanket "we are currently closed for submissions" statement.

If you are close to someone with influence at the press, see if you can have this person recommend you and your manuscript. For example, Accents has published three poetry books by Frank X Walker, and he is one of our bestselling authors. Frank wrote to me to ask if I would read a chapbook manuscript by Yvonne Johnson, a young Affrilachian poet. I agreed to read the manuscript and loved it, and we published her first chapbook, *I Am Woman*.

In the most common case, however, where we have no famous friends or inside connections to a press, the literary power we are left with is our own words.

I remember in 2003 drinking soda made by a local company, with each bottle featuring an anecdote printed on the label. One story that stuck with me was about the owner's daughter, born with one leg shorter than the other. The girl won a school race and recounted the event to her parents, adding, "but I had an advantage...." The parents assumed she had been given a head start, but the girl clarified, "I had to try harder."

I'm sharing this story because, even if it doesn't seem so at the time, winning based solely on the quality and strength of your work is your biggest advantage. If you don't have anyone to recommend you, your work can perform that function better than anything.

Once you identify an appropriate publisher, the next step is to research the press further.

What to Look for in a Publisher

Let me say in advance that there is no perfect publisher. The goal is to choose the best possible home for your work. Here I'll outline a few factors that I consider important, and we'll discuss most of them in detail in later sections.

The first thing to do is to browse the press's **website** and see whom they've already published. The books of a press are its business cards, and the authors of these books are the press's spokespeople. I'd look through the list of authors to see if I know someone personally. If I do, I'd likely try to contact this person and inquire about their experience. You can tell a lot by what they say and also by what they don't say. There is a big difference between a simple note such as "I had a great experience, and I highly recommend them" and something like "Can we talk on the phone about this?" Don't be afraid to ask questions.

Even if you do not recognize any of the **authors**, you can still read the bios and get an idea of their career levels and backgrounds. To me, seeing a diversity of backgrounds and a mixture of established and emerging authors is encouraging news.

Check out the book **covers**. If you dislike the covers you see, there is a good chance that you won't like yours either. At this point you may or may not have an insight into the cover policy of the press. The more similar the covers are in terms of look and feel, the less likely it is that you would have much input. I know a small press that requires the authors to sign a document agreeing to accept whatever cover the press gives them. I also know a small press that asks you to submit your own front cover as part of the deliverables. Most publishers' stance is somewhere in between.

What if the press has no website or any options for **online commerce**? Unless this is a letterpress with special circumstances, I would likely not consider this press an appropriate home for my book. I want my publisher to have a modern, well-maintained, up-to-date website. You decide what is important to you—for me, international reach is of critical value.

Excellent **distribution** is a major check mark for any publisher. Besides their website, where are the books sold? As much as we criticize Amazon, we all want our books listed there, right? Ingram? Whatever replaces Small Press Distribution? Local bookstores, if there are any left in the area?

Whenever I consider a press, its **longevity** gives me confidence. There are no guarantees, of course, and the long-standing presses at one point were brand-new publishers, but if the press has been around for a while, it's more likely that it will continue to exist. Furthermore, speaking as a publisher, even though we never compromised on our books, we did become better after some troubleshooting and trial and error in the first few years. Also, the press' audience, influence and esteem increased with the number of books and the array of authors offering their work to us. That said, I would consider hopping on the ground floor with a new press if I knew the people and had confidence in their grit and competence.

When you see publishers at **book fairs and conferences**, it means three things: (1) you can actually meet the people you would be working with, should your manuscript be selected, (2) you can get an idea of what your book might look like, and (3) you might have a chance for a book signing at their table in the future.

Not all publishers invest time and money in **table events**. I consider a publisher's presence at such occasions a plus, for these events provide excellent networking opportunities for everyone involved. I appreciate the chance to speak with colleagues and research potential venues for my own work. It's inspiring to feel the physical presence of people behind tables, books arranged in front of them.

The publisher's **attention to detail** is an indication of their degree of professionalism. You can surmise volumes of information by examining the way the books look and how well they've been typeset, proofread and edited. If any illustrations or tables are included, how do they look?

Also, it's important that the publisher uses a **quality printer**. If you do not like the paper or the look and feel of the books they are currently publishing, what makes you think you would like the book they publish for you? It does make a difference in the publishing experience and in your relationship with the book after it comes out. You will have to live with this book for the rest of your life, and hopefully beyond.

How well does this publisher **promote** their books, and do they even? Again, the website will give you important information. If you are willing, you can sign up to receive the publisher's mailing list. You will be able to monitor over a period of time how often they publish, what kinds of books they bring out, and what they do to publicize new releases. Additionally, you'll be alerted to any submission opportunities.

How do they **price** their books? This affects you not only as a customer but also as an author. How expensive will it be for you to buy copies of your own book, albeit at an author's discount?

Do this press's books get reviews in high-profile journals—or in any publications, for that matter? Book **reviews** are exceedingly difficult to come by. Few people take the time to write reviews for an ever-decreasing number of outlets. It is nearly impossible to send a book blindly to a reviewer and get a review. That said, certain presses consistently get their books reviewed in prestigious literary journals. This is an excellent indication that your book would get professional attention and proper marketing.

Ideally, the press will have a **good and generous contract** with their authors and reasonable production schedules.

Ideally, they will be responsive and professional and a joy to work with.

And, ideally, you won't have to pay for any of it.

Making a Good First Impression

If you are sending a query, research the press beforehand and let it show in your cover letter. Nothing causes me to delete an email faster than a random note that screams: "I know nothing about your press, I'm just mass mailing with the least effort possible." If you send a query, indicate why you think your book would fit well within the catalog of that publisher. Which books have you enjoyed reading? If you have paid attention to what the press is doing, then there is a better chance that the press will pay attention to your work.

Below are quotes from a few instantly deleted, unsolicited queries I've found in my inbox:

> "To whom it may concern" [likely Katerina Stoykova]
> "I won't include a list with all my credits because I don't want to bore both of us."
> "Feel free to google me."
> "Enjoy!"
> "Your name sounds familiar."
> "To whom it may concern: attached is a document with 50,000 words from a novel."

"Included is my covering letter."

"My excitement could be contained no longer!"

"Choosing 50 pages to send is as impossible as choosing a
child to sacrifice. I've narrowed my sample from XYZ down
to 100 pages of 214."

"Thank you for taking a looksee."

If you are encountering a publisher by browsing a book fair,
take some time to leaf through the books and ask a few questions
about the press and its mission before talking about yourself and
the manuscript you've been trying to place. This is a really good
opportunity for you and a potential publisher to learn about each
other in a professional setting. Both of you have come to this space
with this shared goal in mind and you could have a long (within
reason) and productive conversation.

If you meet a publisher at a social event, unless the occasion
directly calls for it, my recommendation is to not talk shop. It's akin
to opening your mouth to show your broken tooth to a dentist you
just met. That is not to say you should forgo a networking opportu-
nity. Take the publisher's card, tell them that you'll send them an
email, and actually follow up.

A few years ago, I wanted to celebrate my 40th birthday with
writer friends, and I rented the basement of a pizza and beer joint.
Then I proceeded to invite all my Facebook friends. People did
show up. One person whom I'd never met before sat next to me and
immediately approached me about publishing his book. I remem-
ber watching him in disbelief and not even wanting to talk to him
anymore, let alone put forth any effort on behalf of his writing.

And then there is the delicate matter of what we should do
with our publisher friends. Is it an abuse of our friendship to sub-
mit our work to them? The truth is, it could be awkward. I think it
would be harder to ask and also harder to say no. I hope that most

people befriend publishers because they genuinely like them as people and not for any publishing benefits down the line. I'm deeply saddened if I ever get the impression that certain poets want to be my friends because they want me to publish them—it's crushing, actually. But I've experienced the opposite as well. Once in a while a friend would publish a fantastic book with someone else, and I'd say something like "How come you didn't give this book to me?" If I have one piece of advice that is true across the board, it is the following: *Ask your friends to publish you only if you can hear "no" and still keep your friendship intact.*

Factors That Work in Your Favor

In poetry publishing, there are factors that work in your favor and also factors that work against you or, at the very least, do not help.

Note that you do not need to have all boxes checked, though the more, the better.

You are a **first-time author**. Many publishers are excited to forge a relationship with an up-and-coming poet and claim discovery. Additionally, in independent poetry publishing, every sale makes a difference, and first-time authors tend to be more readily supported by their family and friends. Tragically, in many cases after the relatives have bought a book by the author, they consider their job done and don't feel that they need to acquire any subsequent collections.

You have a **large network**. The first people to learn about a particular new book are the author's friends, family, coworkers, colleagues and followers. The more numerous these groups, the better the chance of selling a larger number of copies.

You have a following, an audience or fans, or you are an

influencer. By definition, being an influencer means that a large group of people are swayed by your opinion. Therefore, if you have a new book, it has a good chance of selling well.

The publisher knows you and likes you. In such cases the publisher looks forward to deepening the relationship you have and believes that working with you will be a rewarding experience, possibly for multiple books over time.

You have supported the press in the past; in other words, you have attended events and/or bought books from the press. This signals the publisher that you have a genuine interest in the books that the press publishes, and you do exhibit discernment in the process of looking for a press to publish your work.

Your manuscript is in line with the mission/vision of the press. If the publisher believes that publishing your book supports the long-term goals of the press, you have a better chance of getting published. For example, submitting a novella to Accents in 2019 or a craft book in 2023 had a much better chance to generate excitement among editorial staff than any other genre.

You are a famous author. That works in your favor. One, the press would have a hard time saying no to you, and two, publishing your book could be considered a prestige publication and many young presses need those to grow their credibility and name recognition.

You haven't published in a while. That gives you all the advantages of a first-time author plus the experience of having gone through the process.

Above all, however, what works in your favor the most is having a **killer manuscript**. If the decision-makers love your work, they will make space for it in the schedule and find money in the budget. Such a situation has happened at my press more than a few times. If, while I'm reading a collection, I get the urge to start emailing specific poems to friends or post quotes on social media (which, of course, I would never do without permission), then I need to admit that I'm going to offer this poet a publication, regardless of how many books are already waiting in the queue.

What Doesn't Help

Emailing a manuscript to a press with closed submissions rarely works, virtually never. The only time this strategy may yield results is when you have a good relationship with the decision-makers and they will, indeed, read and consider your manuscript.

Dear Sir letters. I do get these, then roll my eyes and delete the emails without reading to the end. Expressions such as "Dear Sir, Attached is my novel" or "Dear Sir, I have a play I'm looking to publish" show me that the sender knows nothing about my press and I will give them similar consideration.

Almost as bad is when the sender misspells the press's name or the editor's name.

If you are a local author, but you've **never attended any of the press's events** or bought any books, then suddenly one day you want to be published by that same press, your chances won't be great. Generally, an active participant in the local literary community makes for a more visible and engaged author, and at the local and even regional level, a publisher is likely to be aware of your standing in the literary community.

Just as you can research a press and talk to another author about their experience with a particular publisher, the opposite is true, too. If your previous publisher tells your future one that you were difficult to work with or that **you did not promote your book**, then this information is unlikely to help you.

Many may disagree with the next point, but my opinion is that **if you've just published a book**, especially if it is in the same genre, that works against you when you try to publish another one too close behind. I understand that there might be different considerations at play here, such as age, production schedules, accumulated work, etc. However, if poet A has just released a poetry book, I'd be a lot less excited about publishing her instead of someone who hasn't published anything in, say, seven years. My experience is that when a poet publishes books too close together, the readers tend to skip some of the titles. Once two books of mine were released at about the same time, and a good friend asked me, "Can you recommend which one to buy?" She wanted to read only one. She did not even consider buying both. In the next chapter I will discuss promotions at length. Suffice it to say here that marketing a book requires an untold amount of energy and time, and if you've just expended effort promoting a book, it would be difficult to do it again too soon after.

Contests

Over the last decade it has become increasingly common to publish a book through winning a contest. Contests are pervasive and sometimes themed and open to a particular subgenre or population. At times it seems as though there is no other route for publication.

It is wonderful to win a contest, and poets do win. What about the rest of the participants, however? Some presses tend to select more than one manuscript, meaning the winner will receive the monetary award (if such is available) and a few selected others will be offered publication with a standard contract but without the monetary award. Still seems like a win, yes?

Except for rare occasions, it's not free to submit to a contest. Most contests have an entry fee. The presses (or organizations) hosting the contest use the proceeds to crowdsource the upcoming books or simply to keep the press afloat. Consider your fee a donation. Financially speaking, you may be able to claim the fees on your taxes. Also, you can research grant options and/or check if your employer has an allowance for professional development and can contribute money toward fees.

Submitting to contests could get expensive, though. My recommendation is to set a suitable rhythm of revision and submission and to find a way to use the contests instead of letting them use you.

Here are a few of my practices:

1. Once you have a manuscript, do not send it to all contests at once. Manuscripts have ways of changing, shifting, and evolving, and soon you may have a revised manuscript that you wish you'd submitted instead. Thus, do not submit one manuscript to ten places on the same date; submit ten versions of the same manuscript to ten different presses over a period of time.

2. I personally do not submit to paid contests where the objective is for one winning poem to be published in a magazine. My apologies to those who administer these contests, but my budget forces me to pick and choose, and I'd rather pay to submit to book-length contests. I have noticed that the fees to participate are often very similar, though the stakes differ significantly.

3. Set a rhythm. Find out the revision-submission frequency that best matches your creative temperament and personal circumstances. My rhythm is sending to one press, once a month, after a fresh revision (or a fresh consideration that yields no revision). Once a month I review my manuscript-in-progress and see if I want to add or subtract poems or rearrange anything. Then I choose one press and send my manuscript. That way, I know that every month I am offering my best effort.

---

4. Last but not least, I recommend that you submit not only the manuscript on a regular basis but also every non-published poem from it. Why is that a good idea? You don't know how long it will take to find a publisher, to get the book on the schedule and to actually receive it in physical form. In the best of circumstances, it will take a few months, but likely we're talking about a minimum of a year. Once the book is out, the poems in it are no longer "unpublished," and most magazines are looking for only unpublished poems. It is possible to submit a poem and have it accepted and published in a magazine while the manuscript is still in circulation, looking for a home. In my view, the more you publish, the better, since more people will read your work.

Therefore, if you have the time, simultaneously send out both the manuscript and its poems. The most efficient method I have come up with to send out the unpublished poems is as follows:

- Copy/paste the table of contents of your collection in a spreadsheet.
- Identify already-published poems (either in magazines or in books).
- Delete these lines as well as any lines representing pages without poems.
- Submit the remaining poems in the most efficient and emotion-free manner you can and keep every poem in circulation alongside the manuscript as a whole.

Following is an example based on my book *The Porcupine of Mind* (Broadstone Books, 2012). As you can see, I used a top-to-bottom approach for submission decisions. In other words, I did my best to avoid overthinking.

A Pasting of the Entire Table of Contents	Unpublished Poems in Order of Appearance	Magazine	Date
O & I	Kissing the Shell of an Egg	Magazine 1	30-Nov
I enjoy your company	To the Rock	Magazine 1	30-Nov
One Should Exercise Caution; Kissing the Shell of an Egg	When You Kiss a Grape	Magazine 1	30-Nov
To the Rock	The Neighbor	Magazine 1	30-Nov
When You Kiss a Grape	Kissing the Tide, as It Pulls Back	Magazine 1	30-Nov
How long have you been like this?; The Neighbor	A butterfly and I	Journal 2	30-Nov
Kissing the Tide, as It Pulls Back; A butterfly and I	Mouse Monologue	Journal 2	30-Nov
Mouse Monologue	The Superhero Is Moving Out	Journal 2	30-Nov
Wear me, said the word lifesaver; The Kiss of the Stone	Don't you ever get tired of being	Magazine 3	1-Jan
An Hour After	The Fly in My Room	Magazine 3	1-Jan
The Superhero Is Moving Out	To the Row of Tall Candles in the Store	Magazine 3	1-Jan
The Suitcase	How did you get to be so beautiful	Magazine 3	1-Jan
Lullaby	Cumulative	Magazine 3	1-Jan
Don't you ever get tired of being	Love Has Everything	Magazine 3	1-Jan
The Fly in My Room	Kissing a Snowman	Journal 4	5-Jan
To the Row of Tall Candles in the Store	The Visitor	Journal 4	5-Jan
How did you get to be so beautiful	Kissing the Lips of Really Bad News	Magazine 5	5-Jan
Cumulative	In the Water, Under the Bridge	Magazine 5	5-Jan
Love Has Everything	Dear	Magazine 5	5-Jan
Kissing a Snowman	The Hug	Magazine 5	5-Jan

What to Look for in a Contest

As I said earlier, contests are pervasive. Below are a few pointers on what to look for in a contest when choosing where to submit.

- Is it recurring or new? Recurring, long-standing contests are preferable. Administering a contest requires time, commitment and resources and it's easy to give up after just one or two submission periods.
- Do you recognize the names of previous winners/finalists? To me, it would be encouraging if any of my poetry group friends and peers have made it through the selection process. Remember the saying that what goes around, comes around.
- Does the contest list finalists? It's disappointing if you don't win, but wouldn't it be wonderful to know that you came close? Most participants consider it an honor to be listed as a finalist. Plus, if your manuscript is among the top choices, it's an indication that you can ease on revising and start submitting this same version more aggressively.
- Does the press select more than one entry? This is an important factor, since it will drastically increase your chances of getting published. Some contests (rarely, but it does happen) consider all entries for publication. In such cases the contest fee is, in effect, a reading fee. I would definitely submit work if I like the press.
- Have they actually published last contest's winner? If two years later you see on the press's website that they've announced the winner, but have not published the book yet, that may give you an insight into their production rhythm and schedules.
- If they've published the previous winning book, what does it look like?

- What has the press done to market it? Some presses use a portion of the contest fees for modest book tours or other promotions and often advertise that fact in the contest description.
- Who judges the contest? Typically either the press's editors or an invited celebrity judge will select the winner. My (possibly unpopular) opinion is that if the press's editors judge the contest, that's good news. I am not against the celebrity appeal, but I like that the editors trust themselves to choose the work they'll be caretaking and supporting in the years to come.
- Do you like the work of the judge? There is no guarantee that the judge will see your work. Many contests use screeners, and the final judge will receive an agreed-upon number of manuscripts to select from. Let's assume that your work does reach the judge, who likely is an accomplished poet. If you are unfamiliar with the judge's work, I would recommend that you look up their poetry. My belief is that if you do not like the work of the judge, chances are they won't like yours either.

Personal and Professional Goals

Finding a publisher and then getting on a production schedule and then having the book actually published can take a long time and require consistent effort. Being aware of what your goal is will help you decide on a submission strategy.

If you are hoping to launch a long-term literary career or a career in academia, it's worth investing some time in trying to win a contest or having your work selected by a prestigious press. Publishing through either one of these routes (even better if it's a combination of the two) will suddenly swing open doors that lead to good jobs, more publications and paid appearances.

If you already have a job in academia but you are aiming to get tenure, then every publication counts. In this case, perhaps a university press would be a suitable first choice.

If your goal is to have a poetry collection that you can share with friends, family, the literary community and the general public, then small, independent presses are a good match.

If you have a built-in audience (such as a church congregation or podcast listeners) and this is the extent of the audience you aim to reach, then self-publishing might make sense. The same goes if your goal is to preserve your writing and to pass something down to members of your family as a keepsake.

Ultimately, we get what we can, and it might be a good idea to assign a deadline to our attempts. If we've been courting our "dream press" for a long while without any indication of interest on their part, it might be time to cast a wider net. And at some point, actually having the book becomes more important than where it came from.

Let's talk about self-publishing.

To Self-Publish or Not

Consider self-publishing if **you don't want to wait**. With self-publishing you have control over the schedule. You can publish it tomorrow, or for Christmas, or for National Poetry Month, or for Labor Day, or for your own birthday. And sometimes, timing is everything. Often traditional publishing takes years to bring the books to life, and too often by the time the book is out, the author has moved on, has emotionally disconnected from the work, and has already read these poems for years at literary events and now feels compelled to read new work, rather than this same material, albeit in a brand-new book. In poetry, at least, many books are sold at readings, and poets who read from books they are excited about have a lot better chance at making sales and signing copies for fans.

Consider self-publishing if you want to keep tighter creative control over your material. When you sign a contract, you do transfer certain rights to your publisher. There is a certain freedom in retaining all your rights, especially if you want to be able to make creative or business decisions about your work without needing someone else's permission.

Consider self-publishing if you want to keep wider profit margins from your sales. If you self-publish, you'll be able to pocket the portion that the author typically receives, plus the portion that the publisher keeps. Before this section of the book is over, you'll see examples detailing the portioning of the retail price among author, publisher, retailer and distributor that should clarify this point.

It appears that the top three advantages to self-publishing your poetry book are to have control, to increase profits, and to do it right away. Shouldn't everyone self-publish, then? Why go through the effort of finding a press and working with them, especially since nowadays publication technologies are widely available?

Let's examine the point about control. If you are self-publishing your poetry book, you have control over quite a few decisions. You have complete control over the physical appearance of the book, its retail price, the schedule, the printing company, the print run, and the distribution as well as any and all promotional activities. This is a responsibility you may or may not want. If you've had some experience in book publishing, all these decisions may not be too big of a burden. If you are a complete novice, you may want to hire professionals or at the very least ensure you have a trusted advisor to guide you through the process of birthing the book and beyond.

If you are self-publishing for the first time, you may not even be aware of everything you might need help with, and you may end up learning some things the hard way. It's a good idea to read a book on the topic. I recommend that you sit down and talk to other self-published authors about their experiences and borrow as much learning as possible. Be sure to talk to someone who has published in the same genre as you.

So what can a publisher do that you would have difficulty accomplishing by yourself? What advantages does a traditionally-published book have over a self-published one? A big plus is that you have an experienced team on your side. If your work is accepted by a press that is more than a one-person operation, chances are you will work with a series of professionals who will apply their expertise to make your book as successful as possible.

You and the book are eligible for post-publication awards. There are a number of wonderful literary awards for which you or your publisher can submit your book. Most are easy to apply for and typically have a small fee, and some can change your life and career overnight if you win or even if you end up as a finalist. However, you'll notice many of these awards exclude self-published books. I should say that most of these awards exclude chapbooks as well. So part of your decision to self-publish or not will depend on what type of book you're planning to publish. Look up the literary awards no matter what. Even if you are not eligible to submit, you can make a mental list of what to apply for with your next book.

There are subtle (or not-so-subtle) differences in the appearance of traditionally-published books and self-published ones. Unless you are an experienced typesetter and book designer (or you hire one), chances are some people will be able to tell that the book is self-published. Here, again, the difference is blurred when it comes to chapbooks, which are supposed to look unique. But my opinion is that a full-length poetry book should be of standard size and paper, should not go crazy with the fonts and must be perfect bound.

If you are a great poet and luck is on your side, you will be published by a press that will place your book in every bookstore in the country and will ensure NPR interviews and *New York Times* reviews. If you find such a press, do your best to sell a lot of books for them, because your past performance will likely figure into their decision when you send them your next manuscript. In the most realistic case for a poetry press, however, the publisher will make your book available for sale on their website, with online retailers and with local booksellers, but between you and me, you are perfectly capable of doing this yourself, if you're willing to put in the effort.

In my view, the biggest advantage that traditional publishing has over self-publishing is the shared responsibility. If you are like most poets I know, there comes a time when you look back on your older work and … let's say … don't appreciate it as much. If your book was self-published, you may have been the only one making the decisions, and you have nobody with whom to share the responsibility. There is strength in numbers. Comfort, too. Working with a good editor could be both rewarding and enlightening, and I recommend it, no matter what publishing route you take.

What You Can and Cannot Control

To focus your efforts appropriately throughout the process of finding a publisher, it is a worthwhile exercise to clarify what you can and cannot control.

Before the book is picked up, **you have control over** the quality of your work, of committing to a suitable rhythm of revisions and submissions. You own the decision of where to send your work as well as your part of the delicate dance of forging relationships with publishers.

It's always beneficial to consistently put effort into writing and working on your craft. You may or may not be able to move on to another manuscript. Often poets are not able to close a manuscript until it's published.

After the book has been picked up, you have control over the timely delivery of the required materials, reacting quickly to the publisher's requests. Your own attitude and professional behavior are in your control, as well as good communication and proactive efforts to prepare for the book launch and to line up appearances.

Conversely, here are **items and activities out of your control**.

Before the book is picked up, you cannot control the publisher's reaction or their answer to your submission or the speed of this answer.

After the book is under contract, you cannot control the schedule. In most cases, it takes longer than you'd like. You cannot control the retail price, the print quality, the font, and, in large part, the cover. You cannot control the distribution of your book, nor the publisher's marketing efforts.

In most cases there is quite a bit of waiting involved, so how could you use your time wisely? What to do while waiting to get published?

After the book is picked up (and before it's published), it helps to know if the publisher will entertain changes, and if so, what the deadline is. This would afford you one final critical look at the collection closer to publication and give you peace of mind that you've done due diligence, not to mention that you might be able to sneak in a couple of new poems.

If the accepted collection contains any unpublished poems, this is your last chance to submit them to literary magazines since most magazines accept only previously unpublished poems. Online journals might be a more appropriate choice since they typically have shorter publication schedules. You may need to withdraw already-submitted poems to avoid schedule conflicts, meaning if you have a poem under consideration in a magazine that will not be released until after the book is out, then you're expected to withdraw your poem from that magazine.

Finish your marketing plan. Once you have a schedule, you can make actual plans for appearances, readings, signings, etc. In the next section you will be able to read in detail about marketing plans.

What to Watch Out for in a Contract

Upon acceptance, you may need to sign a contract.

One common misconception is that if you sign a contract, that means your book will be published. This is not necessarily the case. Signing a contract means that your manuscript has been taken off the market and the publisher you signed the contract with is the only one who can publish and distribute it. Since the publisher is the one offering you the contract, many things in it work in the publisher's favor. You should be aware of what the contract means and what you are giving up and for how long.

First and foremost, the contract should enumerate **what rights are being granted** from you to the publisher. I'd advise against signing a generic turnover of rights to a publisher without understanding what exactly these rights are. Paper? Audio? Electronic books? Translations? And in what geographic locations? For how long? I've seen contracts where the publisher has added the generic "any other formats not invented as of yet." I would think twice before signing such an agreement. Whenever other formats are invented and the publisher wants to offer your book in these formats, then they can approach you (or your descendants) again with a new contract.

Try to negotiate retaining the right to use individual poems in other projects. This can be addressed by adding (or subtracting) specific language to the contract. If you are publishing a chapbook, make sure you have the right to absorb the poems into a full-length collection. For example, in one of my contracts, the publisher added at my request the following clause: *The exclusivity of the grant is subject to the Author's right to use individual elements from this WORK in future publications without restriction from the PUBLISHER.* This gives me the opportunity to use my own poems from that particular book in future collections or translations, even though the book as a whole is exclusive to that publisher.

Second, you need to know **how (and when) the rights revert back to you**. In other words, there needs to be an exit clause in the contract. Here are a few events that typically trigger "the return of the rights." (This sounds like the title of an action movie, don't you think?)

- If the publisher does not release the book by a certain date specified in the contract. This is the publisher's deadline. Sometimes priorities shuffle in publishing organizations and you do not want your book to keep getting kicked back to the end of the line.
- If the publisher goes out of business, all rights to your work should revert back to you.
- If they do publish the book, but it goes out of print or they otherwise fail to meet customer demand.

Does this contract have an expiration date? In other words, how long is the contract valid? Three years? Seven years? Having a fixed duration for the contract means that the rights will revert back to you upon reaching that date.

Sometimes poets are afraid to ask questions. Please don't be reluctant. Ask for clarifications. Make sure you understand what you are signing. What is the worst that can happen? The publisher could get upset and change their mind and decide not to publish your book? If a publisher would discard you just for asking questions about the contract, that sounds like a red flag. Find another publisher who respects their authors.

The suggestions in the section on contracts do not constitute legal advice and it's always a good idea to consult with an entertainment or copyright lawyer, especially if you feel pressured, rushed or in a high-stakes situation or if you cannot understand the legal language.

What Do You Get in Return

What do you get in return for granting the rights for your book? If you've won a contest, you may receive a monetary award. In rare cases, you may get an advance. More commonly in the poetry world, however, the three things to hope for are free books, royalties and the ability to purchase copies of your own book at a discount. Any of these three items varies from publisher to publisher, but typically free books vary from five to fifty, royalties from 5 percent to 20 percent of the retail price, the discount on author copies varies from 20 percent to 50 percent of the retail price.

These initial free books are your author payment. You can use them any way you wish. You can sell them and keep the money, you can give them away to friends or you can send them out for reviews. My recommendation is to try to sell at least a portion of these copies and then use the money to buy more copies at a discount.

Selling books you've bought at a discount is another way to make a bit of cash. In order for this to work, though, you'll need to engage in direct sales, for as soon as you involve a third party such as a bookstore or an online retailer, the percentages shift, and not in your favor.

The Anatomy of a Book Price

To demonstrate how the profits of a book sale get parceled out, let's examine three scenarios.

Assumptions about the book:

$20.00 retail price
$3.00 printing cost
$2.00 royalty (10 percent of retail price)
$11.00 distribution (55 percent of retail price—yes, not that uncommon!)
$8.00 bookstore discount (40 percent of retail price is the standard)

Direct Sales from the Publisher's Website

Publisher clears retail price, less royalties, less printing cost.
$20–$3–$2 = $15

Bookstore Sales

Publisher clears retail, less royalties, less printing cost, less bookstore discount.
$20–$2–$3–$8 = $7

Sales on Amazon or Through a Distributor

Publisher clears retail, less royalties, less printing cost, less distributor discount.
$20–$2–$3–$11 = $4

In all these scenarios the author receives constant royalties. The publisher's cut varies significantly depending on the sales option. In short, if you like small, independent publishers and want them to stay in business and continue their work, buy books directly.

If you have self-published your collection, you will, indeed, receive a higher percentage from each sale.

Self-Publishing: Direct Sales

Self-published author clears retail price, less printing cost.
$20–$3 = $17

Self-Publishing: Bookstore Sales

Self-published author clears retail, less printing cost, less bookstore discount.
$20–$3–$8 = $9

Self-Publishing: Sales on Amazon or Through a Distributor

Self-published author clears retail, less printing cost, less distributor discount
$20–$3–$11 = $6

Paid Publication

Note that the above example covered only "cost of goods sold," so to say. There is no provision for the expenses of producing the book, such as typesetting, cover design, the editor's work, software, computer upgrades, etc.

Certain publishers request a sum of money to cover part or all of the publication expenses. This is a somewhat controversial issue. On the one hand, it would be wonderful to have the press cover all expenses in advance and recover these costs through book sales or some other means—contest fees, grants, donations, etc. Not all presses employ such practices and may find themselves in situations where they pay for everything, never to fully recover their investment. This is their choice, and the author carries no responsibility for it.

That said, if you like a particular small press, and you're in a position to be able to help with the costs, I see nothing wrong with that. You don't have to do it up front, either. Buying your own book at the author's discount is a way to help the publisher recoup expenses. Also keep in mind that the press is more likely to work with you again on another book if they have not lost money on your previous one.

As for your return, it is not impossible to make money from book sales, but don't count on it to pay your rent. Besides royalties, money from your book could come your way through paid appearances and readings or teaching classes or conducting workshops. Additionally, an indirect financial benefit is that having a poetry book published makes you eligible for a wider set of jobs in academic and other settings.

What If the Press Does Not Offer You a Contract?

It is not too unusual for some small presses to not use formal contracts. There is no need to feel exposed or unsafe if you are not given a contract. There are benefits to that as well. You won't need to ask for permission to reuse or repurpose your work, and that could give you significant freedom and convenience down the line.

To avoid misunderstandings and clarify assumptions, you can try to get the most important information in writing. For example, you could initiate an email in which you outline the basics: "Am I understanding correctly that I need to deliver the manuscript by May 12, and you'll send me 15 copies when the book is out? And I'll be able to buy more copies at a 50 percent discount?"

Qualities Needed at This Stage

Ability to hear "no" without being destroyed by it. For good or bad, rejections are the rule rather than the exception when submitting unsolicited literary work for publication. Remember: (1) No means no. If the press passed on your work, it's not a good idea to write to ask why, to try to convince them to change their mind, or to make them feel bad for hurting your feelings. (2) It's not personal. Even if they accept work that you consider inferior to yours, or even if they are publishing your frenemy, they did not reject you to ruin your day. (3) Rejection is nothing to be ashamed of. In truth, if publishing were easy, it wouldn't be nearly as attractive. (4) Rejection is nothing to be proud of either. In my view, it's best to be neutral about it and not invest strong emotions on either side of the spectrum.

Ability to dream. In part this requires faith in one's own work, emotional maturity and a lack of fear of success. Persistence helps, too: sticking with your rhythm of revision and submission in the face of rejections and the onslaught of daily life.

PART 5

Promotion

Mic Check

Where are we now in the process? Quite far along, I hope. My assumption is that at this point you have assembled and edited a manuscript, this manuscript has been selected by a press of your choice, you have signed a contract, and now you're waiting for the book to be published. As in the previous stages, there is work to be done here as well. In this section I've attempted to outline in some detail certain actions and prep work that will guide you along.

One way to naturally divide the promotional activities is marketing before the book has been published, marketing soon after the book has been published, and marketing long after the book has become reality. The aforementioned respectively translates to

- preparing for the book to arrive;
- actively promoting and caretaking the book; and
- reminding your followers that such a book exists.

In any of these stages, you want to make sure you're engaging in stage-appropriate activities. For example, if you start your publicity planning after the book is out, it's very much like starting to cook after the guests have arrived. You should have planned and cooked dinner beforehand.

Your Role Versus the Publisher's Role

Whether your publisher has a marketing department or the entire press is a one-person show, my recommendation is to have a conversation with someone at the press regarding the marketing and promotion of your book. It is reasonable to ask questions. Here are some examples:

> When is the targeted release date of my book?
> Do I need to coordinate with you for the book announcement and/or cover reveal?
> Are you planning a book launch or other readings I can participate in?
> Are you blasting out a press release?
> Are you sending any copies for reviews, and if so, where?
> Are you submitting the book for post-publication awards?
> Can you put me in touch with anyone who can interview me for a magazine, a radio show, etc.?
> Are you attending any book fairs and/or conferences where I could do a book signing at your table?

In most cases your publisher will welcome such a conversation, because together you can accomplish more, and a concerted effort avoids duplication of time and resources. If you have drafted your own marketing plan, you can show it to your publisher so they can see what you're already planning to do yourself. They might be able to support your activities in some way or have follow-up ideas. And since they've probably been through the process a number of times, they may advise you as to what activities have the potential to yield good results.

In the best-case scenario, your publisher will do much of the promotion. They may be able to reach reviewers and venues that you have no access to. If so, that's great. It's like having wind in your sails. Still, even if you have a major publisher's marketing machine working for you, you will need to put in some effort as well, especially if you're early in your career.

It would be disappointing to discover that your publisher is uninterested in investing time or resources to promote your book. Still, that kind of information is valuable, since it will give you a clear idea of where you stand—everything is up to you.

When is the best time to have this conversation? As early as six months before publication day and up to three months before the book is available would give you sufficient time to schedule publicity events.

Obtaining Blurbs for Your Book

A blurb is a written endorsement, typically the length of a paragraph or two, in which one poet (or a person of influence) praises another poet's work. This blurb can then be used for marketing purposes and book promotions.

It is common practice to include several endorsements on the back cover of the book and also to add them to press releases or to feature them on the author's website.

Who endorses your book is a statement of literary power and connections. The fact that [insert popular poet's name here] has taken the time to read your book, has provided several sentences of praise and has signed their name under it means something and does impress people. Fame in the poetry world is contained within the poetry world, however, and I can almost guarantee that your cousin who doesn't read poetry has heard of neither blurbs nor the blurbers.

So how important are blurbs anyway?

The truth is that you do want to obtain a few for your upcoming book, especially if it's a full-length work. Since featuring blurbs is a common practice, not having them will stand out.

If I were to see a contemporary American full-length collection without endorsements, it would signal to me that this book might be self-published by someone who did not quite understand the standard publishing procedures. Furthermore, a blank back cover is a missed opportunity to communicate how this work fits within the literary conversation.

How should you go about securing blurbs and what is important to know?

Communicate with your publisher and follow their lead. They might ask you to deliver several blurbs by a certain date, or if you are very early in your career, the publisher may offer to approach well-known authors on your behalf. In the latter case, you don't need to do anything.

If securing the blurbs is up to you, then it's a good idea to spend some time considering whom you might ask. Most people ask their mentors, creative writing teachers, workshop leaders, peers and poet friends further in their careers.

The most important consideration is whose words you would like to see on the back cover. Whose praise would be meaningful to you? This would be your first choice. If you are able to approach these people, send them an email that lets them know that you have an upcoming book you're thrilled about and that having their words would mean a lot to you. Give them a graceful opportunity to decline as well as a deadline as far in the future as you can. Also, ask them to let you know either way.

Here is an actual email I used to ask for a blurb for my latest poetry book.

Hey _____,

I have a poetry book coming out early next year from _____.

_____

Would you possibly consider writing a blurb for my book? It would be a great honor to have your endorsement. If you agree to do it, I would need the blurb by the end of April.

If you are unable to, I completely understand, but please let me know either way.

Eesh. I cringe at the thought of adding more work to your plate ... yet I'm sending you an email with the request.

Make no mistake, requesting blurbs is an imposition. It does create an inconvenience and a burden in someone's schedule. Well-known poets get asked to provide blurbs so often that many eventually announce a no-blurbs, no-exceptions policy, and if you bump into such a policy, know that it's not a personal rejection.

No sweat if you cannot get [superstar poet's name here] to endorse your book. Actually having the blurbs is much more important than who wrote them. Think of your top three favorite poetry books. Without looking them up, can you answer the question of who blurbed them?

If you receive a positive answer from a potential blurber, do send them a copy of your manuscript and a deadline. Some blurbers prefer to receive an actual printout; others are happy with an email attachment. Do communicate with your publisher, as they might want you to send out a typeset, watermarked version of the book, and others would have no preference.

At times it may make sense to look beyond the literary community for blurbs. For example, Emily R. Grosholz's book *Childhood* deals with motherhood and adoption, with heavy focus on peace and the tragic consequences of war. Emily was able to obtain a blurb by Tadatoshi Akiba, past president of Mayors for Peace and past mayor of Hiroshima, which beautifully supports the book and its message. Here is an excerpt from that blurb:

Childhood by Emily Grosholz reminds me of how delightful, invigorating, and at the same time humbling my experience of parenthood

---

was.... One reason why so many Japanese and American people made the commitment to "morally adopt" thousands of children orphaned by the atomic bomb that destroyed Hiroshima might have been because they knew these truths, and felt the sentiments that *Childhood* so beautifully captured.

Tadatoshi Akiba is not a literary figure, but his personal connection to parenthood, adoption, war and peace provide valuable support for Emily Grosholz's book.

Sometimes authors who have already published books can reuse and apply more generic-sounding previous praise to a newer book. Poet Andrew Merton did this for his fourth collection, *Killer Poems*. He selected non-book-specific quotes from the blurbs for his previous three books. The result was as follows:

PRAISE FOR ANDREW MERTON'S POETRY

This poet pinpoints the extraordinary in the day to day; he makes the reader see things anew, and even when they appear tawdry and tough, they are rich and sweet. The calm and gentle voice of these poems is nevertheless fierce in its focus on life, aging, disappointment and death, and that makes for the tremendous tension that keeps each poem taut with drama, inviting from the very first line, and powerfully moving until its conclusion.
—JOHN SKOYLES

In Andrew Merton's view of poetry, brevity is the soul of wisdom. His poems are compact. He likes plenty of white space around some image or pithy utterance.... Merton is like some elderly neighbor, someone we pass on the street for years without a second look, someone who—when we finally exchange a few sentences—seems to be thinking and worrying about many of the same things we have, someone we would like to spend more time with from now on.
—CHARLES SIMIC

Merton mixes a playful surrealism with the knack of capturing both the hilarious and the deadly, and pulls off the visual psychologist's trick of making the familiar strange and puzzling. All of this is delivered in that most serious of all modes, a graceful sense of humor.

—RORY BRENNAN

Echoing the work of Kenneth Koch, Billy Collins and Albert Goldbarth, here comes another poet primed to tickle and provoke. Simultaneously wise and hilarious, Merton somehow plumbs issues like depression, self-loathing, regret, grief and finds its funny lining.

—JULIA SHIPLEY

If Andy Merton's poems were baseball caps, they wouldn't say "Make America Great Again," they'd say "Make America Sane Again."

—DAVID RIVARD

Creating a Marketing Plan

As I've mentioned already, in book publishing, as well as for any project delivery, it's a great idea to develop a plan. A marketing plan contains the intersection of what you are able to do and what you are willing to do as well as specific steps to accomplish it. There is a Bulgarian expression: *it is one thing to want to do it, yet another to be able to do it, and third and fourth is to actually do it.*

If we follow the outline of R. Buttle's online article "Five Essential Elements of a Marketing Plan for a Small Business" as it pertains to a new book, the result might look something like this five-point plan of action.

Clarify Your Marketing Goals and Objectives

Let's start with a few examples:

My goal for my first poetry book was to make everyone I knew aware that I had published a book, that I had become an author. I deliberately excluded sales figures from my goal. I locked my focus on building awareness that such a book existed and that I had written it. As a matter of fact, this was a really good goal for two reasons. First, awareness does not directly and immediately translate into book sales, but I believe that eventually it does. And second, intuitively, I was focusing on something within my control.

I do not need to tell you that spending time and effort on what is in your control is much more productive than spilling strength beyond your sphere of influence. You have probably heard author Steven Covey say a little something about this matter. It was in my control to send announcements to everyone on my list. To organize and publicize a book launch party. To mail a few copies as gifts. To participate in all readings I could. To make sure my website was updated. I'm happy to report that *The Air Around the Butterfly* had two reprints in its first year.

For my second book, I had a different goal. I had the ambition to make sure my publisher recovered his financial investment. He was my friend, and I had heard him say that he'd lost money on each of his books. I wanted his experience with my book to be different, so I worked to sell as many copies as possible by participating in as many readings and events as possible. I'm happy to report that *The Porcupine of Mind* was the first poetry book on which Broadstone Books made a profit.

For my latest Bulgarian-language book, the goal was so well defined that my publisher included it on the website as part of the book description: *I asked myself: What do I want for this book? And the answer is clear. I want* American Delicacies *to be part of the Bulgarian literary conversation. To have an opportunity to add my voice to the choir. Even the mere thought ignites joy in me.*

The above examples illustrate three different goals for three different books. Your marketing goal is personal to you and reflects your personal needs and ambitions. It might be something like:

- Sell X number of books.
- Have a reading in every county near your city.
- Have the book reviewed in the *New York Times* or at least in the local paper.
- Win the National Book Award.

Or you could aim for an alloy of goals. In any case, I'd recommend that you spend some time clarifying your goals for yourself, since they directly affect the activities you'll plan and follow up on and the metrics you'll use to evaluate the results.

Define Your Target Audience

These are the people you would like to make aware of your book's availability. These are the people who would likely buy it, review it, talk about it, or recommend it to others.

For my first book, my target audience was everyone who personally knows me in both the United States and in Bulgaria.

For my second book, my main target audience was people who attend readings and literary events, since they were the most likely group to buy books.

What makes sense in your case? **Whom would you like to reach?** Who would be a natural fit? For example, Accents author Jude Lally suffers from Friedreich's Ataxia, and a lot of the poems in his three collections address the challenges of living with the disease. Part of his audience includes other patients and their families. For years, Jude attended the yearly Friedreich's Ataxia conference, where he would set up a table to offer his books and to meet some of his potential readers face to face.

Who could you team up with? My Bulgarian-language book *Second Skin* discusses the issue of domestic violence from the perspective of a child. My publisher sent out copies to domestic violence organizations throughout the country and invited them to the book launch, which a few did, in fact, attend. Inspired by the book, one of the domestic violence organizations launched its own initiative, *Healing Words*, in which they gave anonymous online space for survivors of domestic violence to share their stories.

You may ask, "Well, can I just have a wide target audience? Everyone who reads poetry, for example?"

In theory that makes sense, but in reality, you reach more people when you focus your target. Plus, the results naturally spill over into the generic catch-all category of poetry readers.

Tap into the Experience of Others

Observe authors in the same genre (and beyond) who have been successful in book marketing. Look to these people for examples of what is customary, what is possible, what are the best practices, and decide what looks interesting to you. If you are able to schedule a sit-down conversation with any of these authors, do so. You can ask questions to determine which specific activities (aka tactics) have been the most beneficial. You can also assess if these authors would entertain teaming up with you for a joint event, a reading, etc. Even if you are not able to talk to these poets, you can still observe them and adopt a few of their tactics.

In general, think who might be able to help you. Who could be an ally in this process? A worthwhile exercise is to build a list and then contact a few of these individuals or organizations. It is perfectly acceptable to contact them even without having a specific idea in mind. You could call and say something like "I wanted to let you know that I have a new book coming out, and I think it would be wonderful if we could collaborate in some way. Would you be open to it?"

After doing the due diligence of researching specific tactics and based on your answers, goals, priorities and availability, you can then fill in the specifics. Start contacting community organizers for appearances, radio hosts for interviews, venues for a book launch, etc. List specific events and assign actual dates.

Develop Your Budget and Timeline

Two questions need to be answered here: "How much does it cost? And how long does this reasonably take?"

"This poetry business could get expensive," a friend once said to me at a conference. It's true. Often, we need to balance opportunities and their return on investment. Notice that this return does not always translate into cold, hard cash. As it pertains to poetry, the concept is more of a joke.

You may or may not need to budget for events, gas money and travel, but one mandatory expense will be buying author's copies for yourself.

Estimate how many books you need for events, gifts, direct sales, etc., then add 10–20 extra copies to keep in stock for opportunities that pop up unplanned. Likely you will need to buy the books from your publisher, and hopefully you can do that at a good discount. Some bigger publishers will simply give you the phone number of a warehouse to call for ordering books, and you'll have to pay for them in advance. Smaller presses might offer you an arrangement where you pay for the books after you sell them. Having a conversation with your publisher might be worthwhile to come up with a win-win solution, especially if buying a large number of books creates difficulty for you. In any case, it's very difficult to sell books if you do not have copies with you, and moving product is a common goal between you and your publisher.

Learn the turnaround time to obtain books from your press in order to plan ahead. Some presses keep stock readily available, while others print on demand, and it may be weeks before you are able to receive new copies. It is disappointing to miss out on sales just because you don't have any books.

Keep track of how many books you have available at home with you. At Accents, we periodically receive panicked calls from authors who are about to go to a reading just to discover that they're out of books and want us to bring copies in an emergency.

How Long Should You Keep Up This Effort?

The journey from a pile of poems to a published book is long and rife with opportunities to give up along the way—or postpone, which, in effect, could mean the same thing. Also, the skills and personality traits you need to progress from a pile of poems to an ordered book are different than those you need to find a publisher, and yet different than the skills you need to let people know about your book, to offer it for sale and to accept a credit card payment.

For many poets, the promotion stretch of the journey is simultaneously gratifying and sobering, inspiring and discouraging.

All this is to say that book promotions take energy and emotion. Keeping up a marketing push can be tiring, so it's a good idea to pace yourself. A word of warning: If you take a longer break, it will be difficult to resume the effort with the same intensity and enthusiasm, so think about what level of promotional activities is manageable and sustainable in your schedule for as long as possible.

I don't want to give you a timeline prescription, though most poets refer to their books as "my new book" during the first year, then shift to using the expression "my latest book" thereafter. If you are applying to a book fair, they consider only books published in the previous calendar year. The requirements are similar when submitting for awards. So your most productive efforts will be within the first year following publication. After a year, chances are the sales will have slowed down, and everyone who needs to know about the book will have learned about it.

Within this year you can schedule periods of more intense promotion interspersed with periods of rest. Not only do you need to pace yourself, you also need to pace the demands you place on the attention from your audience. You cannot schedule three readings in the same city in the same week. But you can schedule three readings in the same city three months apart.

Below you will find examples of two "sprints"—two scheduled periods of intense promotional activities.

For my book *Second Skin*, I committed to a 30-day sprint. My goal was every day for a month to do one thing for the book, no matter how big or small. One day the "thing" was a book launch; another day, just a social media post or an email to a culture vulture. Once the month elapsed, I took a break.

Accents author Pat Williams Owen, upon the release of *Orion's Belt at the End of the Drive*, committed to daily personalized emails to three people from her target audience. In these emails she'd catch them up on her life, inquire about theirs, then share her news about the new book and send them a link to purchase it, if so desired. Pat was kind enough to send out the publisher's link, so I was able to monitor her progress. During this stretch of time, she was one of our best-selling authors. She was willing to keep up this effort until she went through her entire contact list.

Putting a timeline on your efforts helps you not only to contain and focus your efforts but also to move on with your life. Other matters need attending to, other books need writing. Life goes on.

Announcing the Book

Spend some time considering who should learn that you've published a book, not only because they'd like to read it but for various other reasons too, even if it's just because they'd be happy for you. I divide the people who would want to know into two broad categories:

    1. People you know personally. This list includes, but is not limited to, family and friends, coworkers (past and current), neighbors, writer friends and acquaintances, including mentors, schoolmates, college roommates, fraternity/sorority buddies, your twelve-step program support group, the members of boards you serve on, childhood friends, social media followers, etc. In other words, all your personal networks.

    2. People you don't know well or at all. This list might contain professional organizations relating to the topic of the book, media representatives for local and regional newspapers and radio stations, a list of influencers to whom you'd like to send the book as a gift, organizers of literary events of all kinds, members of reading groups.

Be exhaustive and deliberate in writing out each category. It's worth the effort, as you are making an important investment in your career. You're building your writer's contact network, and you'll be able to use this information not only for this but also for every subsequent book you publish. With every release you will be able to expand your reach and do so faster, because you will have done much of the pre-work on a previous release.

Building your writer's network, book promotions, etc., will help you receive invitations, make acquaintances, and afford you opportunities to share your work with audiences. Success begets success in writing, as in anything else, so the more opportunities you find for yourself, the easier it will become for more publicity to find you.

So what to do with these lists of contacts? Wait until the time is right—such as the book becoming available or the preorder link becoming active—then contact each category in the appropriate way. Some of them will require a personal phone call, text or email; others will be best reached via Facebook post; and, for others, mass mailing would be enough.

Aggregate as many relevant email addresses as possible in a personal mailing list. Create it early, be deliberate, keep it current, and add new contacts as you come across them. I'm not talking about having a flashy "professional" newsletter that would keep them informed about your personal and professional successes. I suggest a warmer, more modest, low-effort approach. You can still send emails to dozens, if not hundreds, of people at a time. Make sure you use the bcc option to protect your contacts' privacy.

Upon the availability or the orderability of the book, let everyone know (1) you have a new book, (2) you are very excited about it, (3) they can buy it via (list methods and venues) and (4) they are invited to a book launch or other scheduled events.

Readings

There is a rule of thumb: "Poetry books are sold at readings." In my experience as a writer, publisher and attendee, I'm willing to confirm that this is true. So let's discuss the various poetry readings that you can benefit from.

Book Launch

If your publisher wants to organize a book launch, allow them to do so and support their efforts. If you are on your own on this, no worries: you can totally handle a book launch. It is something like a birthday celebration for your book. Try to hold this event as soon as the book is released or shortly thereafter. While you can (and should) have multiple readings from your book, you can have only one book launch, so you can (and should) go all out. Plan a big event. Have a designated photographer, videographer or live-feed person. If possible, bring simple refreshments. Most important, make sure the book is available for sale. You could assign a sales-person—your spouse or a friend—or you could invite a represen-tative of your publisher to sell the books. You could even invite a bookstore to set up a table. *Who is handling the sales?* is an import-ant question, as it has both financial and relationship implications. Typically, the party organizing the event also handles the sales, but other arrangements are possible as well.

Keep the focus on yourself and the book. I've attended book launches where the author invites other poets to read before them. I personally advise against such a practice, unless there are other considerations calling for it. The crowd has gathered to hear *you* read from *your* book. This is not meant to be a joint reading; you can (and should) have joint readings in subsequent weeks, months and years. The goal of a book launch is to celebrate the release of a book to a broad audience, to sell as many copies as possible and to feel good about the accomplishment.

Send invitations to people you like and who want to see you succeed—even if they are not big readers. Every subsequent event will be attended just by those who want to listen to poetry, ergo the proverbial struggle for audiences in poetry readings. Generally, there are no random people at such events.

If the book you're launching is not your first one, it will behoove you to bring a few copies of all your previous books. The attendees will have a chance to complete their collection or buy extra copies of the books they've purchased before and enjoyed so much that they now want to gift them to others. Do not underesti-mate the power of impulse purchases!

Joint Events

Look around to see who else has a new book in need of promotion. Ideally, this person (or persons) will live in the same city or within driving distance. You can then join forces, connections and audiences to have one or more joint readings. You can even partner up for a book tour. In the poetry world, having several readings and interviews scheduled during a particular time period shortly after the initial release of the book could be considered a book tour.

The person you have combined forces with does not need to be a poet or an author, for that matter. They could be an artist, an actor, or a musician, and you could organize a multi-genre event with a wide degree of appeal and originality. Together, you can showcase multiple art forms in the same venue or at the same event. For example, Accents author Christopher McCurry, with the help of gallery director Jeanette Tesmer, organized an exhibition in which specific poems by various poets were matched up with paintings by local artists. The exhibition was on display at the Living Arts & Science Center (Lexington, Kentucky) for several months. Some time ago, an artist friend organized an event in which he created new paintings live while several other poets and I read original work.

Reading Series

Tap into already existing reading series in your area and beyond. This is a great way to utilize established venues with (often) loyal audiences and present your work there. The advantage is that you won't need to do lots of event promotion and legwork yourself, yet you'll read your poetry to new ears. Normally you need to contact the reading series organizers well in advance so that they can schedule your appearance during a time period beneficial to you.

For example, being invited to read in a prestigious, well-attended reading series two weeks before the book arrives from the printer would be a missed opportunity for sales. There is no guarantee that you'll sell any books even if you do have a book in hand, but at least it won't be a scheduling snafu.

I want to stress that when a new book comes out, you should read from the book rather than new work. You might be excited about the poem you wrote that afternoon, but if you have a new book, you have a responsibility to it. Plus, if you don't read from the new book, and your publisher is in the audience, they will likely not be happy. I understand that it might have taken you years to place the book and await its turn in the production schedule, and by the time you hold it in your hands you may have moved on to something different. Nevertheless, read from the book. Also, read the poems as if you're excited about them, as if you like them, as if you're proud to have written them and to have had them published. Often people from the audience will buy a book because they want some of that excitement, pride, and sense of accomplishment.

Other Ideas for Readings

Traveling could be a wonderful way to plug into another literary community. You may or may not be able to secure appearances as a featured reader, but even if you don't have a major role, you can still read from the book at an open mic or simply attend an event to listen and network with other poets.

Open mics are among the most common literary events in the United States and are readily accessible to almost anyone who wants to share some form of creative work. If you have a new book, you can read a poem and promote it in that way.

At times, a milestone needs to be highlighted, and that could be accomplished by an **anniversary** reading. Years ago, I decided to celebrate the twenty-year anniversary of immigrating to the United States with a poetry reading. It was important and meaningful to me. I'm already looking forward to the thirty-year mark, and I plan to organize another reading.

At times you can come across **seemingly unrelated events** which could stand a poem or two—for example, art gallery openings or a presidential inauguration. On such occasions, poetry has a supporting role but still can give you and your book some valuable visibility. So read through the calendar of cultural events and see if you can approach someone for a moment in the spotlight.

Performing Your Own Poetry

All this talk about reading in front of audiences might seem intimidating. It helps if you are the kind of person who enjoys performing for crowds and gets energized by attention. "Personality sells books," I've heard my mentor Molly Peacock say. It's true, but only for those members of the audience who are not there for the poetry itself. There will be those who recognize good poetry and will want to buy the book for its literary value, so how skilled you are at reading won't matter to them. And there will be those who will want to buy the book because they are attracted by the personality and charisma of the reader. Another bit of Molly's advice was that you're allowed to be yourself at the mic. Hearing that helped me a lot when I first started reading in front of audiences. The good news is that most often, you are the harshest critic of your own performance.

The four most important elements in reading poetry are:

1. Make sure that everyone can hear you.
2. Speak 20–30 percent more slowly than normal.

3. Enunciate.
4. Do not go over the allotted time.

Ensuring these four items will go a long way in having a successful reading. Practicing at open mics and other lower-stakes events may help you build confidence for solo readings. Observe others to learn from their performances, events, choices of material, and from the listeners' responses to the readings as well.

Still, things feel different from the other side of the mic. And sometimes there is no mic, and you have to project your voice beyond your comfort zone. And sometimes there is background noise, especially if you're reading at a bar. Sometimes there is not much of an audience. If that's the case, when you start the reading, don't comment on it, and don't show disappointment. And sometimes you read with a superstar author, and everyone gushes over them, not you. And there is the rare occasion that you might start crying during your own reading. Don't apologize. Instead, say something like "Wow, I didn't expect that." Or even try a joke such as "If you cry at your own poem, it must be good." And sometimes people leave during your performance, or chew gum, or don't applaud. Ignore them and read to the person or persons listening. It gets easier with practice. Readings can be fun and rewarding, I promise, despite the litany of things that could go wrong.

Interviews

Interviews are an effective way to emphasize what you want everyone to know about you and your book, a wonderful excuse to brag, namedrop, or otherwise put your best foot forward. Some interview ideas include radio, television, blogs, YouTube channels, podcasts, magazines and newspapers. The opportunities are diverse and readily available. If there is no interest from the mainstream media, you still have options. Your publisher may include a Q&A with you on their website. At the very least, talk to a writer friend and exchange interview questions and post the interviews on your respective blogs or even have a friend interview you and post the conversation on your own blog.

Interviews take time and thought, but what else could be more important when a new book is out?

Teaching Classes

Offering a class on a topic related to the book is a way to draw attention to both yourself and to the book. A few examples: I am the editor of *Bigger Than They Appear: Anthology of Very Short Poems*, so I offered a class on writing free-form poems of up to 50 words. Meg Files is the author of *A Hollow, Muscular Organ*, a novella about the dissolution of a marriage due to infidelity. She offered a class on risky writing. Showcase a skill you've mastered during the writing of your book. If you've written a book of persona poems, give a talk on writing persona poems. If so desired, include a physical or electronic copy of the book in the price of the class or just remind the participants that the book is available for sale.

Utilizing Social Media

Social media is your friend in book marketing. With virtually no time and effort, you can keep the book in the forefront of readers' minds. You can post news about the book or photos of individual poems, you can invite your contacts to events or share links to reviews, and there are many, many other options for publicity.

During the time period surrounding a book release, you can make the book cover your current profile photo, so that all your family, acquaintances and followers will be aware that you have a new book and can see what it looks like. In a way, your public persona is in service to the book.

That said, keep yourself a human being on social media instead of transforming into a lean, mean, marketing machine. People can—and will—tune you out. Very quickly you'll notice that your book promotion posts gather less and less attention. Therefore, do your best to make sure others talk about your book as well. When my first poetry collection came out, I met with Donna Ison, a friend who had recently published her first novel, *The Miracle of Myrtle: Saint Gone Wild*, and over lunch we discussed book publicity. Then she gave me a great piece of marketing advice: "Put your book in the hands of people who will talk about it."

It's best if these people are influencers, since they have the ability to instantly reach large audiences. Still, anyone who has read your book and writes a Goodreads review or makes a public endorsement on social media can be considered a win.

The best kind of publicity is unsolicited recommendations and praise—public, if possible, from an influencer. Reviews are a form of this, and we'll address reviews later.

Make a short list (or a longer one, if you can afford it) of people to whom you'd like to mail books as strategic gifts. To this list you could add several poets whose work you admire, and you would consider it an honor if they owned a copy of your book. These could be your mentors, individuals whom you're grateful to, or people who could help you in some way, should they love the book. Sometimes wonderful things happen. For example, Wendy Jett, the author of the mixed genre book *Girl*, sent a copy to a theater director friend who, upon reading it, became interested in producing the story as a play.

Web Presence

What kind of web presence should you have? Create a website? Or a blog? Isn't social media enough?

Good use of social media will take you far, but that space, by its nature, is dynamic. Consider a website or a blog more of a static platform where you showcase professional information about yourself that you'd like for everyone to know. Artful, fancy websites are great, but a simple low-cost blog would do the same job. Whatever you choose, make sure that it's easy to update and keep up to date. It's better to have a homemade blog that you can update by yourself than a professionally made website that you do not have access to.

It goes without saying that right before the release of a new book, you should make sure your website or blog features current and relevant information.

Another easy and unobtrusive way to keep building awareness about your book is to have it listed in your email signature. In this case, every time you send an email, automatically you let the recipient know about your books. You could add links for more information and ordering.

No marketing opportunity is too big or too small. Few things are as invisible as a poetry book. Poets can't be choosers.

Reviews

If your publisher has the influence, connections and means to secure book reviews, that's very good news for you. Bask in the glory and gratitude for your good luck. For the rest of us, book reviews are hard to come by and normally involve some legwork.

Can't you send a book to a magazine and they will just magically review it? I wish it were that easy. Over the years I've had zero success with this approach for any and all books I've mailed out, so I've stopped cold calling and adopted more targeted and hands-on practices.

In order to have a review published, you need (1) a reviewer and (2) an outlet.

Do you have friends who write reviews or wouldn't mind trying their hand at it? You can start with that crowd and ask around who might be willing to write a review. It would be a kind gesture if you offered them a reviewer's copy, meaning a free print copy of your book. Your publisher likely has a few books set aside for that purpose, so feel free to ask if they'd mail a copy to the reviewer.

The reviewer might have their own idea of where to submit the review or they may have a publication they already work with. If so, that's wonderful—your work is done. If not, then you or the reviewer can start querying journals. The good news is that nowadays there is an increasing number of outlets that are willing to consider and publish reviews. Many journals have added a "Submit Review" button to their submittable pages. The process is very much like sending out individual poems to magazines. In fact, as you are submitting individual poems, keep track of the journals that accept reviews as well.

Certain professional organizations review books by their members. For example, the Kentucky State Poetry Society reviews new poetry books by KSPS members in their *Pegasus* journal. What does your local, regional, or state poetry society offer? What about other organizations you belong to or could pursue a membership in?

Post-Publication Awards

Being listed as a finalist for an award and, even better, winning it can propel your book's visibility beyond the local and regional audiences. Additionally, these honors renew the interest in a particular title and keep it fresh in the minds of the people who meant to buy it months ago but for one reason or another didn't.

Obviously, the more prestigious the award, the better, but any degree of good news could be used as an excuse to send an email update or to initiate a series of updates on social media or to schedule a special reading.

Some of these post-publication awards have application fees, and submitting can quicky get expensive, but many awards are free to apply for. It is up to you to determine what you're comfortable with and how much work and research you are willing to invest. In either case you will need to submit physical copies. Your publisher might be willing to contribute a few or even spearhead the initiative. It's worth asking.

Distribution and Sales

Where should your book be sold? The short answer is "every place that will have it." Here your publisher's distribution channels come into play because the wider they are, the more accessible your book will be. Ideally, your press would have worldwide distribution, which makes your book orderable from any and all online retailers that carry books. I'm happy to say that this is not all that impossible to achieve with today's technology, and some of the on-demand printers automatically provide their books with such distribution. Once the book is orderable, any bookstore can stock up on physical copies as well. Even small, independent presses such as Accents have global reach.

In case your publisher doesn't offer wide distribution, you want to make sure that at the very least your book is available on the publisher's website and on your own website as well. Even if you don't know how to add a credit card button to your page, you can still write a sentence inviting those who want to purchase a signed copy to send you an email.

Hit up as many local bookstores in your region as you can. Many of them have it as part of their mission to support local authors and would gladly put your book on their shelves. If they are unwilling to buy copies, you can offer several on consignment. Even if the books never get sold, even if they get lost, even if they get sold but you never receive the money from the sales, still, your book was on the shelf of a bookstore, and everyone who looked at this shelf saw your book. That also is marketing.

Sometimes unusual opportunities arise. For example, the owner of a popular Middle Eastern fast-food restaurant in my city read my first book and loved it. She suggested that they offer it for sale by the counter, along with some spices, olives and jams. Of course I agreed, and my book sold out every time I brought fresh batches of copies. Another time, a friend with a flower shop stocked my books, and they also sold well there. Consider who would carry your book and where potential readers could lay eyes on it. You can work out some mutually beneficial financial arrangement, though you should know that the typical bookstore discount is 40 percent. That's why, if your publisher gives you less than 40 percent discount, it may be unprofitable for you to distribute the book yourself.

Book Fairs

A few times a year, opportunities arise for participation in book fairs and book fair-like events. On these occasions you will be expected to be present at a table and sell your own books. Here are some hard-learned best practices that could help you sell books and also have a good time.

First, make your table a welcoming space. Bring an attractive, bright tablecloth, and make a creative arrangement of the books across the table. Less is more, which is to say fewer is better, meaning, do not pile 50 copies on the table but rather scatter five or six. Add your business cards. If you have swag, such as bookmarks or candy, they can contribute to the color and character of the table.

Make sure you have a means to accept credit cards. Currently several companies offer simple devices that you can plug into your phone to allow you to swipe credit cards and an associated app will deposit sales proceeds directly into your bank account.

Provide change for cash sales. Bring a small cash box in which you can keep change and dollar bills. Have a convenient and quick way to log purchases for your records.

Design a sign-up sheet where people can write their email address to keep in touch or to learn about future books you publish. Make sure you bring several sheets of paper, plus pens.

If your health allows it, stand up, and stay up as much as possible. Make eye contact with the people walking by. Initiate conversations. You don't need to do anything beyond "Hi, how are you today?" If the person responds, feel free to ask them something about themselves. If it's a writers' conference book fair, you can ask them about the genre they write in, or if they have a reading, or if they are participating in a panel.

Feel free to engage the potential customer with information about the books on the table. Some of the approaches I use are "I am the author of this book. It is a book about ..." or "I'd be happy to tell you about these books. Please let me know if you have questions" or simply "Please feel free to look around."

For the most part it feels like cold calling, and it could be discouraging—even exhausting at times. A sense of humor will help and so will not taking anything personally. Those who make the most sales manage to maintain high energy until the very end, keep a welcoming and unassuming smile on their faces and don't let up. If for no other reason, smile because you have a book, and you've been given an opportunity to showcase it. Furthermore, I've noticed that at book fairs most of the sales happen toward the end of the event. If you assume there won't be any sales and leave early, you might miss out.

Rites of Passage

Certain initiations and rites of passage happen to everyone, so instead of considering them a defeat, you could choose to feel good about the experience and scratch it from the "it was bound to happen" list. Here are a few common discouraging experiences:

- No sales at a reading or a book fair.
- Virtually no audience at a reading besides your partner and the organizers.
- General lack of interest in your new book by people outside the writing/reading community.
- No follow-up questions (or even feigned interest) when you tell a friend that you have a new book.
- A slowdown in the writing of new work. Most poets I know go through a few months to a year of difficulty starting new writing projects.

You don't have to toughen up or become cynical, but again, do learn to not take anything personally. The truth is that your book and every activity associated with it is a lot more important to you than to anyone else. Be aware of which aspects of the promotions and sales are in your control and which are not.

The Issue of Control

It's in your control to let people know that you have a new book, to give them information about where they can buy it, to invite them to an event, to create a welcoming space for everyone in attendance, to treat the audience kindly and without expectation for them to actually make a purchase, to make it easy for them to buy a copy, should they decide to do so, to speak positively about your book and to remember that it represents your best effort for the time period of its writing, editing and publishing.

It's not in your control whether someone will attend or enjoy your event, whether they'll stay to the end, whether someone will buy your book, read it and appreciate it, and whether they'll talk about your book, and if so, what they will say.

In other words, the book has been *released*, with all implications of that word.

What If You Hate It and Want to Hide?

I truly hope that your book publication is a joyful experience that fills you with pride and desire to share your accomplishment with the world. I'm sorry to say, however, for some poets the reality might be a bit different.

By the time your book has been published, you may have divorced yourself from it. You may have written new poems, or you may have taken more classes and learned better ways to write, arrange or edit. You may have come up with a better title. You may hate the cover and not be able to do anything about it. Meanwhile the book unrelentingly traveled through production, and now you are faced with a box of your author's copies—this evidence of your imperfect and eager creativity. You'd much rather hide it and start over. You'd much prefer that nobody sees it, much less reads it. Or the book might contain references to personal information you felt safe sharing while writing the poems but wish you could redact now that you feel exposed.

Under these circumstances, how do you develop a functioning relationship with your own book? How do you promote it and talk about it?

First of all, you are not the only one experiencing this phenomenon. Sooner or later, to one degree or another, this happens to most poets. Outgrowing your own writing is not a shameful secret but rather an uncomfortable inconvenience if it happens too close to publication.

So how do you promote a book you would rather hide?

Learn to speak about it positively. Find aspects of the content and/or the publication experience that you do enjoy and focus on them when talking about the book.

Second, select five or so poems that you do like and feature the same poems at every reading or publicity opportunity.

Third, if you have a good working relationship with your publisher, you can have a conversation with them about your struggle. They might have advice or even work with you to keep you out of situations that feel uncomfortable. This honest approach of communicating with your publisher will work to your benefit in the long run and is much better than dropping off the face of the earth without explanation.

The most important thing to remember is that you cannot abandon your book, especially not in such a vulnerable and important stage. If you do not promote your book, not only will the book itself suffer, but you may also damage your relationship with the publisher.

Publisher Relations

It's one thing to become an author of a press, yet another to remain in a good working relationship with them. Here is what you can do to improve your chances of having a subsequent book picked up.

- Be prompt in answering emails. True, your publisher may regularly take their time in getting back to you, but you don't have this luxury.
- Deliver materials on time. Often publishing is fraught with delays, but do your best to avoid contributing to these delays. If anything comes up, do communicate early and openly.
- Make the most out of your current publication. Whether it's a stapled chapbook or a full-length collection from a prestigious press, your actions (or the lack thereof) influence its success. The way you stand behind your current book speaks volumes not just to your current publisher but also to other potential publishers. At times I'd see a poet who puts tremendous heart, effort and time into promoting her book, and I can't help but think that I'd love to have this person as an author at my press. I might even tell them so.
- Send direct sales to your publisher rather than to online retailers. There will be people who will ask you about your preferred way for them to buy your book. Then, unless you're selling your own copy, share the ordering link to your book on the publisher's website. It makes a tremendous financial difference to your publisher and none to you. Chances are that they will notice and will be grateful.
- Never complain publicly. There will be something during the publication process that you will find annoying. If it's a big issue, have an open discussion with your publisher. If it's

a small issue, let it go. And never bad mouth your publisher on social media or in other public spaces. It's not a good look, and other publishers might notice. When a press takes you on as an author, they get not only your manuscript but also your personality, and every publisher knows that.

• Make sure you acknowledge and express gratitude at readings. During your book launch, or your press releases, or social media announcements, there will be opportunities to mention the press and the team that helped bring the book into physical existence. To not do so is impolite, at the very least.

• If you are organizing joint readings, you could choose to invite other authors from the same press, thus netting more sales for your publisher. This kind of consideration costs you nothing, though it goes a long way toward goodwill and solid relationships, and it doesn't go unnoticed.

• If you decide to publish your next book with someone else, do let your previous publisher know. You can send them a courtesy email or tell them in person. They'll appreciate not learning through a book announcement that you've forged a relationship with another press.

After the Book Has Been Out
for Some Time

You published a book. You worked hard to promote it. Even under the best of circumstances, however, and sooner than you'd like, the conversation surrounding your poetry collection will die down, the public's focus will naturally shift to other books, authors and activities. At that point you can still tastefully bring attention to your book and periodically remind your audience that such a collection exists and is still available for purchase. Here are a few ideas on how to do this.

Whenever you publish new books, let the older ones share the limelight. Refer to them when you discuss the latest. Bring them to book-selling events, and, if appropriate, read at least one poem from the older books.

On your blog and/or social media you can **feature timely poems**. For example, it's Mother's Day, and in your older collection you have a poem about your mother. You share this poem, along with your book's title and a link to purchase the book if it is still available. You can also share vintage poems related to current events. Certain poems turn out to be prophetic. For example, my poem "O & I" from *The Porcupine of Mind* is a love story between a woman and a single cell organism. When the coronavirus pandemic began, the poem added a few other layers of meaning.

You could **continue submitting poems** from your older book to anthologies and magazines that accept previously published material—that is, if your contract allows for it.

I believe it's a good idea to celebrate or at least to **acknowledge book anniversaries**. Wouldn't it be wonderful to hold an in-person or virtual reading to mark ten years since the release of your first book?

Sadly, sometimes books go out of print. Publishers go out of business. You rarely have a say when a decision is made to discontinue a title once all copies have been sold. The good news is that, under such circumstances, all rights revert to you, and you can republish the book with another press or with a different cover or arrangement. If you do not want to republish the book in its entirety, you can select your best poems and use them in your next book or in a new-and-selected volume in the future.

Marketing Yourself
Versus Marketing Your Book

Hopefully, you will write and publish more than one book, so think long term during your book promotions. You should be able to leverage the learning, the process and the contacts for every subsequent release. The benefits are highly cumulative. People who have bought your current book are a lot more likely to buy your next one(s). With this group you're no longer cold calling but actually following up with an existing customer.

While publishing a book is a true accomplishment, it is you who ultimately needs to be marketed as a writer. Your collection is a sample of what you're capable of, and you may write more books after this one. So cultivating a following is important. Know who your audience is and where and how to reach them so you can contact them again in the future.

In other words, it should get easier.

Qualities Needed at This Stage

Detachment. Your book is not you. If someone shows no interest in it or decides not to buy it, that is not a personal rejection. And even if it were a personal rejection, so what?

Sense of Humor. The entire process will be easier if you don't go through it with a life-or-death kind of attitude, but keep amused, delighted and grateful and manage to extract learning every step of the way.

Afterword

Thank you for reading this book. I hope some of these processes, suggestions and opinions have been of use to you. I would love to hear your feedback or ideas for edits, additions to or subtractions from this material.

This is the first edition, so I hope to continue improving the content with updates in the future. Please let me know about your experience with the guide and how you're doing with your stack of poems.

Email me anytime at poetrybookguide@gmail.com with feedback, questions or comments.

Acknowledgments

My deepest gratitude to all my mentors, students and colleagues and to everyone who serves the field of poetry. Special acknowledgment to my mentors at the Naslund-Mann Graduate School of Writing: Kathleen Driskell, Greg Pape, Molly Peacock, Jeanie Thompson, Debra Kang Dean, Maureen Morehead and Dianne Aprile.

Thanks to all members of Poezia writing group in Lexington, Kentucky, for the thousands of hours spent together poring over each other's work.

Thanks to the 34 brave poets who signed up for the Poetry Book Boot Camp workshops in 2022 and 2023, during which the first version of this book was drafted and edited. Thanks to everyone who was willing to share their experience in support of the material in this book.

Special thanks to Libby Falk Jones for reading an earlier draft of this book in its entirety and providing valuable feedback and to Daniel Klemer for his help in editing and proofreading the work of this sometimes-insecure second-language writer.

Thanks to the Kentucky Foundation for Women for awarding me a grant in support of this book.

Thanks to my husband Bill Schloemer for the loving, safe and supportive space to write and thrive.

Appendix: Extras

Obstacles, or How to Not Write Your Book

We spent quite a bit of time discussing how to conceive, arrange, edit, publish and promote a poetry book. We zoomed in on good practices for every one of these stages. Still, I feel that we need to highlight a few potential pitfalls. So how can you trip on your way to creating and publishing a poetry book? Below I've exposed seven distinct obstacles.

Obstacle One: Getting Stuck in One of the Stages

In order to conceive, arrange, edit, publish and sell a book, you need to employ a spectrum of different skills and engage in vastly diverse activities. Most people I know feel more comfortable with some and shy away from others.

In the conception stage, where you focus your material into one or more themes, you can be tripped up by simply not knowing how to proceed. Facing your own pile of poems—diverse in subjects, quality or editing stages—could overwhelm and discourage you. Sentiments such as "I don't know what to do" and "I don't know where to start" may leave you blocked and perpetually postponing the first step.

In the arranging stage, you need to order your poems in a representative and meaningful way. The number of potential combinations is staggering and can be discouraging. If you haven't done enough work in the conception stage, it will be harder to decide which poems to include, not to mention in what order. You may feel stuck due to a lack of clarity. In reality, you need to have just enough clarity to take the next step. In the process of arranging, clarity develops by clarifying, through trial and error. Clarity begets clarity.

In the editing stage, there is the danger of getting lost in the details and allowing the editing process to take an inordinate amount of time. There is the danger of getting trapped in perfectionism and pursuing too much feedback from peers and mentors to either seek validation that the work is good enough to start submitting or to find an excuse for continuing to edit and not move forward toward publication.

While pursuing a press for your book, you can still get stuck because the publishing efforts could serve as a distraction from writing and pose a roadblock on your general path as a writer. Being overly focused on finding a home for a manuscript can prevent you from further revising it or moving on to another project, not to mention the insidious voice suggesting that since nobody wants to publish this book, why bother writing another? Furthermore, I've noticed that the vast majority of poets experience a slowdown in writing, ranging from a few months to a year (or even longer) after publication. To me, this makes sense, because after publication, different skills, energies and even personality traits take center stage. Typically, the more outwardly directed aspects of one's personality are not the ones closing the door to write in solitude.

In the marketing stage, when the book is about to be released, and in the period following publication, you may struggle to achieve balance, balance between marketing and writing, privacy and visibility. How much of your day-to-day life and what portion of your social media output should be hijacked by marketing activities and calls to action? True, the book is already on the market at this point, but you still have responsibilities, as you are a major part of its support system.

Every one of the five stages requires different energies, experiences, and various facets of your poetic persona. Each facet relies on distinct personality traits and skills. We all have our own strengths, so we need to be willing to admit that there may be some areas where we need further education and support.

Obstacle Two: Not Making Your Book a Priority

In my experience, if you want to finish a book, at some point you'll have to make it a priority, even if only for a stretch of time. That means focusing on your book over everything else, including spending time with children, cooking food, doing laundry, getting regular sleep, pursuing well-paying jobs, caretaking relationships, etc. Does that sound extreme? Perhaps, but I've seen too many poets reach the verge of finishing a book just to get distracted by misfortunes or opportunities or just day-to-day life.

Publishing a book is a result of a long series of victories—some of them more visible than others. There is a gauntlet of challenges, and each time you advance, you've achieved a victory. These tests are posed sequentially, and a poet can trip on any of them. A few of these tests concern the actual writing and the uncompromising quality of the work. Some have to do with personal boundaries, others with insecurities, time management, or the ability to ask and to receive. For these reasons, I say that publishing a book is not only a victory but also a graduation to another level of relating to one's work and self.

Obstacle Three: Lacking a Plan

Without a plan, it is difficult to make anything a priority. Furthermore, with a good plan you'll be aware of the next step in the process at all times. That next step will vary from stage to stage, but if you're always clear on what is to follow, you will feel much less anxiety during more challenging activities. A manageable next step need not be a giant leap or a revolutionary book architecture. It could be as seamless and minute as swapping out a poem or relineating a stanza.

Obstacle Four: Waiting Too Long

Procrastinating on a project holds real, specific dangers for your work. You might lose interest and completely move on from the subject. Since you will likely continue to read, write and work on your craft, you may start writing in a completely different way. On many occasions, I've seen poets attempting to combine in one manuscript poems with differing energies, style, even skill levels, and it rarely works. They know it, too, so eventually most poets leave behind the old work and start over. So you may fall into the vicious cycle of gearing up work on your book and not following through. It's not time wasted—no time working on your writing could be considered wasted—but what would you think of a gardener who sows seeds and cares for the plants yet doesn't harvest the fruit? If this feels familiar, think back—what made you stop? At what stage did you give up? I'm not saying that waiting is not the right thing for some manuscripts or in certain situations, but make sure you have enough awareness of your reasons for tabling a project.

Moreover, while you're waiting, you're not the only one changing. The world itself may move on, and that could affect the relevancy of the writing. I've seen this with political poems using specific markers and sentiments that date the work.

Obstacle Five: Deciding Not to Publish

Publishing can be intimidating because it brings a sense of complete vulnerability and loss of control. Often poetry books contain personal material or divulge emotional information, and it's understandable why the author might feel exposed. Dread of offending exes, friends, bosses, or relatives can also paralyze us at this stage. When people are afraid, they try to control the environment as well as the opinion of others about themselves or certain events. Once the book is published, control is irrevocably lost. In the poetry world I've noticed (and experienced) tension between the need for privacy and the need for sharing. Dance with your own level of comfort. My opinion is rather extreme. I believe that that nothing is sacred in literature. Everything is fair game to write about and subsequently publish.

Obstacle Six: Wanting to Be Sure You'll Succeed Before Investing Effort

Craft aside, writing poetry is nontrivial emotional labor—spending all this time, sinking in all this effort, going through all this anguish. Shaping your material into a book can really bring into focus past trauma and unresolved issues that have found their way into your poems. Self-sabotage might sneak its way in through insidious questions: "Why do it to yourself? Is it worth it? What if nobody wants to publish it? And even if somebody decides to publish it, what if nobody notices it? Worse yet, what if the book finds readers but nobody likes it?" My advice is to acknowledge that risks exist, but instead of indulging in self-doubt, focus on the reasons for wanting to write and publish your work as well as on the potential benefits for doing so.

Furthermore, make sure you understand the difference between wanting to write a book and wanting to publish a book—you have control over one and not the other. Ultimately, you need to *want* to do it. The easiest thing is to not try.

Obstacle Seven: Waiting for the Right Time

Wouldn't it be wonderful if your obligations magically fell away and you were left with the time—and hopefully the means—to focus on your writing? However, life doesn't pause, years go by, opportunities close their doors. I've heard many reasons in favor of waiting, and every one of them sounds perfectly legitimate: "When I retire, I'll have the time to be a writer; when the children start school, I'll finish my manuscript; during the summer vacation, I will put my collection together...."

Time is a choice. For as long as we are alive and of sound mind, we actually choose not to write and instead attend to other issues of our lives. I'm not saying that this is not the correct thing to do, I'm saying that we choose to go to the office, or to have children, or to go out for coffee with our cousins, or to sleep in. Hour by hour we decide what to do with our time, and often we choose to not write. Let me say that it is easier to not write than to write. Therefore, if all of a sudden you were left with a large block of time for writing, that doesn't mean that you'd actually write. Writing is not a matter of time but a matter of space. If you haven't cultivated space in your head for writing, then likely you won't write, even if you do have the time.

So what can we do? Here is what I believe.

Even during busy periods, it is possible to set aside time to stay connected to writing in some constructive way on a (nearly) daily basis. A few examples: ten minutes of editing, five minutes of free-writing, two minutes of researching, writing one sentence a day before sleep. During one impossibly packed period of my life, for an entire month, my only commitment was to spend one minute a day thinking about my project. I would actually set a timer to complete the assignment.

Cultivating such a consistent, committed relationship with our writing helps us to be much more productive when we do receive the comparatively rare gifts of longer stretches of time to devote to a project. Without this pre-work, having extra time can actually feel overwhelming with all its possibilities and blank spaces, pressures and expectations.

Writing in Sprints

I believe in **writing in sprints**. I don't believe in committing to overly ambitious, unaccomplishable goals. Egos love to sabotage us by setting us up with goals that are doomed to fail so we have an excuse to give up. Often these goals are all-or-nothing goals. They may sound something like "From now on, for the rest of my life, I'll write three hours a day" or "I'll read two books a week, no matter what." Our goals should not be depressing and discouraging but rather inspiring and energizing. I've studied volumes on goal setting and experimented with various programs, videos and advice. What has worked best for me is to set **monthly creative goals** for myself and to list them among my other professional and more mundane obligations. A creative goal cannot exist in a vacuum. Writing happens in the midst of living, and we need to do everything in parallel. I have found that without setting specific creative goals, I accomplish a lot less. Also, in my case, at least, weekly creative goals do not work so well. Creativity is a longer-term beast, and in order to accomplish something—writing-related or in general—I need to be able to outline longer-term goals and subdivide them into accountable monthly accomplishments.

Evaluating my various monthly commitments, to-dos and other life happenings and deciding on the most productive creative goal for that month I call *setting up a sprint.*

What would a sprint look like? Below are several examples.

- Spend 30 minutes on my writing five times a week during January.
- Polish the drafts in the drafts folder and submit them for publication in February.
- Translate a poem a day during March.
- During April, finish the second draft of XYZ manuscript.

Toward the end of the month—the end of the sprint—I'd reassess and give myself a new creative goal for the following month. Reassessing your goals and recommitting to them refreshes them and helps you avoid forgetting what you actually want to do. The important thing is to set a rhythm of reviewing and planning.

The Book Horrors

We write poems. We work hard at our craft. We learn. We get feedback from respected mentors. We edit. We send work out for publication. It gets rejected. We are discouraged. We refuse to give up. We send work out again. Eventually, several poems get picked up in various journals. Maybe one even gets nominated for a Pushcart prize. We are beside ourselves with happiness and so proud. We tell our parents (unless the work is about them and may upset them), we tell our friends, we rejoice and celebrate. We are encouraged and optimistic, and we decide to start sending a book-length collection out. We have our pick of small and large presses, contests galore and open reading periods. So we send.

Fast forward some time. The collection looks nothing like the one you started with, the title has changed twice, you have ordered and reordered the poems an unreasonable number of times. You have restructured it at least three times based on brilliant suggestions by writer-friends who were kind enough to read and comment. Your friends have all published collections already, have had readings and book signings, and you are wondering what you are doing wrong, since, of course, you are a much better poet.

But one day, as they say in Bulgaria, the sun will rise on your street and you will get a call, or more likely an email, that your poetry book manuscript was picked up by a small press that would love to bring your work into the world. This will make you as happy as you can possibly bear to be happy, and you will be ecstatic for a very long time—a very long time, because you will be surprised to learn that it takes a press, on average, more than a year to edit and publish your manuscript and add it for sale on their website. You will be thrilled and will look forward to holding the book in your hand ... until you get *The Book Horrors*.

The Book Horrors arrive about a week before the release date. They take the form of chills up your spine and severe anxiety, attacks of shame and the sinking feeling that, by publishing this book, you are making the biggest mistake of your life. Why did you have to do this in the first place? You are about to ruin any chance of a career in poetry you might have otherwise had. You should have arranged it differently. And since the manuscript got typeset, you wrote five other poems that would go great in the book. And now you know for a fact that the book could have been better. And the first poem? Is it really that strong? What will your mentor say? She never liked that poem. And what if nobody comes to the book launch party? (Side note—don't worry. Your best friends and your closest enemies will be there, and that typically makes for enough of a crowd.) What if nobody buys it? (Side note—don't worry, you won't sell too many. Drop every expectation about the number of books sold.) What if nobody notices it? (Side note—don't worry. Chances are a couple of friends will do kind reviews on blogs or in local papers.)

The Book Horrors don't stay with you 24/7. They come unexpectedly and punch you in the gut, make you want to hide because you feel exposed. Your first poetry book is coming out. You are hoping that it will change your life. (Side note—don't worry. It will change your life. But not the way you think.) It will change you, and then you will change your life. You have to step out there and own your book, your poems, even the front cover, which you may or may not love. You need to live up to the blurbs that your mentors wrote. And that's a lot of responsibility and a lot of work. You also need to realize that this book is a snapshot of the best you were capable of on the date your book was accepted. If you could have done better, you would have. Now it's time to devote your efforts to a new project.

And *The Book Horrors* do go away—shortly after the book launch party, after you fully realize and accept that the publication of this book was a big deal only for you and maybe also for your publisher. For everyone else it was a relatively unemotional and distant event. Then *The Book Horrors* might be replaced with a sense of letdown, which only a new project can help shake off. And yes, when you publish it, *The Book Horrors* will be back. And that's okay.

A Comprehensive Example

As promised, I'm including the entire text of Libby Falk Jones's write-up on her experience arranging her fourth poetry collection:

ORGANIZING A POETRY COLLECTION: MY EXPERIENCE

My full-length collection of poems, tentatively titled *Southern Ladyspeak*, includes 84 pages of poems written over a period of about 20 years. My subjects are my girlhood in southern Louisiana in the 1950s and 60s, as well as my (and other southern women's) adulthood, including marriage, motherhood, and the deaths of parents.

Reading through the collection, I saw various possibilities for organizing. I'm drawn to poetry books with sections, as I believe groupings can offer coherence while also allowing a reader to breathe between chunks of poems. Sorting the poems roughly by subject, I came up with four sections: girlhood, lady-hood, marriage/motherhood, loss/grief. Sorting the poems, I was able to make the sections about equal length, and also to create smaller groupings within each section.

Reading through the poems in the order I'd created, I saw problems. There was too much overlap from section to section, especially in the last two sections. The fourth section, in particular, bothered me. It was shorter than the other three (16 vs. 21 pages) and included poems that, though they spoke to loss and grief, were from girlhood and marriage. None of the sections seemed clearly focused. In fact, I was unable to find a good title for each section; I'd just used roman numerals. I worried that readers would spend time wondering why the sections existed, rather than engaging with the poems.

Since the section on loss and grief didn't seem to hold together, I tried integrating those poems into the three other sections. Those seemed to have some integrity: girlhood, the Southern lady, marriage/motherhood. The three sections were also about equal. But reading through this order, I was still bothered. Some of the poems in each of the sections seemed to be put there arbitrarily. Naming the sections still didn't make sense; all the sections included poems exploring growing up as a southern female. Perhaps the poems in the second section, focusing on the Southern lady, could be integrated into the section on marriage and motherhood? But some of those poems drew primarily on material from girlhood. And if I broke the book into two sections, the girlhood section would be two-thirds of the total. I didn't have enough poems on marriage and motherhood to constitute half the book. I had more than enough poems for the collection, so generating several more just to fill out a category didn't appeal to me.

My solution? Let go of structuring into sections and work instead on creating resonance between small sets of poems, pairs and triplets, while maintaining a rough time sequence, with poems drawing on childhood coming earlier, those focusing on marriage and motherhood coming later. In creating pairings and triplets, I looked for common subjects or approaches and also tried for variety in form and tone. Reading through the first rough order I created, I was able to fine-tune placement, moving a few poems a place or two. It was freeing not to have to think about the rationale for and coherence of a section, and instead to concentrate on the reader's experience of a couple or three pages. From one pair/triplet to the next, there was a gradual progression. I thought the experience of reading would be like stepping on one stone, hesitating, then stepping on another. There was a path, a beginning and an ending, through this world of Southern females. Katerina suggested paying particular attention to the relationship between the first and last poems in a collection. I was pleased with this pairing: the first poem brought an adult perspective to one experience in childhood, and the last poem returned the adult speaker again to childhood, but with a focus on the experience of writing poems about the past.

I wanted to let some time pass before finalizing the structure, so I set this project aside. Bringing fresh eyes to the project now, I think that the structure I created makes sense. But I find I'm still attracted to the idea of having sections. I don't want the collection to overwhelm readers. Perhaps try for more, rather than fewer, sections—say five or six? Might that allow more coherent groupings? Seems worth a try. I'll gather my pages, sort them, and then read through the piles. I'll keep open to possibilities, recognizing that no version of the structure will be "perfect." Focus, resonance, and variety—those are my goals. I have waiting a reader, a poet friend who's also revising her collection, who'll consider both versions and give me feedback. Dancing with words is always a pleasure.

Bonus Parting Words

I want to share with you a few quotes on the subject of writing that are included in my book, *Bird on a Windowsill* (Publishing House Signs, 2017, bilingual).

* * *

If you don't write when you don't have time for it, you won't write when you do have time for it.

Writing is not a matter of time but a matter of space. If you don't keep space in your head for writing, you won't write even if you have the time.

Talking about writing is not writing, in the same way talking about the gym is not exercising.

To write, you need more courage than time.

Muses love leisure.

* * *

The Four Stages of Writer's Block:

Stage I. I want to write, but I can't.

Stage II. I have to write, but I can't.

Stage III. I don't want to write, but I have to.

Stage IV. I don't have time for writing … and, honestly, I don't feel like writing.

* * *

Poetry is a connection to a change within you.

As we change, our writing changes too. You cannot write the same poem twice.

At the end of your life, it won't matter how much you've written but how much you've changed.

The ultimate goal of writing is forgiveness.

Our books resemble us.

Be nice to your children. They may grow up to be writers.

* * *

Writing is personal work for public consumption.

The audience likes its poets vulnerable.

Writing to impress others is the surest way to pretentious mediocrity.

The inability to objectively judge your own art is a special form of mercy.

Writing can be seasonal. Liking your own writing can also be seasonal.

* * *

Two half poems don't make a whole one.

More words do not make for a bigger poem.

Adjectives are carbs, verbs are protein.

If a poem is well made, that doesn't necessarily make it interesting.

---

* * *

Tell me the language you keep silent in, so I know how to listen. Do you have something to say or do you simply want to talk?

If you want to write, keep silent. The more often you repeat something, the more certain it is you won't write it.

When you notice that your thoughts are smarter than you, start writing them down.

Notes

Part 1

Writing in Series

Introduction to *The Man Pages*, as well as links to the various commands, can be found here: https://man7.org/linux/man-pages/index.html.

Chapbooks or Full-Length Collections?

I would like to give credit to poet Leatha Kendrick. Some of the thoughts in this section arose in a conversation she and I had before we co-taught "How to Put Together a Poetry Chapbook Manuscript" at the Carnegie Center for Literacy and Learning in Lexington, Kentucky, in 2010.

Part 2

Combinations and Permutations

Online calculator: https://www.calculator.net/permutation-and-combination-calculator.html.

The Iterative Approach

Charles G. Cobb, *The Project Manager's Guide to Mastering Agile: Principles and Practices for an Adaptive Approach* (John Wiley & Sons, 2023).

Part 3

Forgive Me For a Few Personal Paragraphs

The pilot I'm referring to is Rumen Radev, president of Bulgaria since 2017.

Part 4

Creating a Marketing Plan

R. Buttle's article can be found here:
https://www.forbes.com/sites/rhettbuttle/2021/01/12/five-essential-elements-of-a-marketing-plan-for-a-small-businesses.

Animus Foundation and link to the page with their *Healing Words* initiative:
https://animusassociation.org/dumite-lekuvat/.

Bibliography

The material in this book stems from a combination of diverse and seemingly unrelated experiences. I want to share with you several books that I've enjoyed and have helped me along the way.

David Allen, *Getting Things Done: The Art of Stress-Free Productivity* (Penguin, 2015).

James Clear, *Atomic Habits: An Easy and Proven Way to Build Good Habits and Break Bad Ones* (Random House Business, 2015).

Richard Goodman, *The Soul of Creative Writing* (Transaction, 2008).

Tom C. Hunley, *The Poetry Gymnasium: 110 Proven Exercises to Shape Your Best Verse* (McFarland, 2019).

Josh Kaufman, *The Personal MBA 10th Anniversary Edition* (Portfolio, 2020).

Jeffrey Levine. *The Poetry Manuscript: Arts and Crafts.* October 12, 2011. https://jeffreyelevine.com/, https://jeffreyelevine.com/2011/10/12/on-making-the-poetry-manuscript/.

Jay Conrad Levinston, Rick Frishman, Michael Larsen, and David Hancock, *Guerrilla Marketing for Writers: 100 No-Cost, Low-Cost Weapons for Selling Your Work* (Morgan James, 2010).

James Longenbach, *The Art of the Poetic Line* (Graywolf Press, 2007).

Mary Oliver, *A Poetry Handbook: A Prose Guide to Understanding and Writing Poetry* (Ecco, 1994).

Molly Peacock, *How to Read a Poem ... and Start a Poetry Circle* (Diane, 1999).

Frederick Smock, *Craft-Talk: On Writing Poetry* (Wind Publications, 2010).

Index

Index

Index

Index

Printed in the USA
CPSIA information can be obtained
at www.ICGtesting.com
LVHW091923041124
795688LV00034B/1088